IN THE COOLING TWILIGHT

In the Cooling Twilight

Essays

ED MEEK

BROKEN TRIBE PRESS

ADVANCE PRAISE

"Ed Meek has provided readers with a rich compendium of insightful, intimate, and evocative essays in his latest book, *In the Cooling Twilight*. I've known Meek as a marvelous short story writer so this is an unexpected and welcome turn on his ongoing literary journey. *Luck* was one of favorite fiction collections, and this newest outing confirms his protean ability to work exceptionally in any genre."

—Michael C. Keith, author of *Insomnia 11*
and *Methods of Repair*

"With the precision of a poet and the compassion of a memoirist, Ed Meek illuminates the quiet dramas of ordinary life. In the *Cooling Twilight* traces the arc of a life—from boyhood skirmishes in schoolyards to the fragile intimacies of fatherhood, from idealism kindled in the tumult of the '60s to the small, luminous rituals of middle age. With wry humor Meek explores the tender intersections of memory, identity, and time. These essays do not merely recount—they reveal the familiar in a gentle and profound light. This is an eloquent and deeply personal collection."

—Steve Glines, writer and publisher,
author of *Poplar Hill*

CONTENTS

AFFECTION

A friend of mine was holding my son in her arms and she said, "babies are so sensual." The more I've thought about it, the more I think what she said was true. Babies _are_ sensual. They love being held, hugged and kissed. They love being tickled. They love baths, and pools and beaches--the water, the sun and the sand. They love to roll around and wrestle on the couch, the rug, the grass. Like dolphins, they seem to enjoy the feel of life.

The company my wife works for had an office party. It was a casual affair with a buffet table, an open bar and a small band. Children were invited so I brought our son Eddie. He'd just turned three. My wife introduced my son and me to her boss and I was a little surprised when the guy swept Eddie up, gave him a hug, inhaled deeply and said, "Ah, they smell delicious at his age." He went on to say that he had two young children himself.

I may be a sensitive guy, but I was a little taken aback by the demonstrative actions of my wife's boss. Not that I actually went as far as to actually communicate to him how I was feeling at the time. If I had, I might have said, "Hey it's okay for me to be affectionate with my son, but you don't even know him so knock it off." At the same time, I could empathize with his impulse. I can understand why anyone would want to show Eddie affection. He's a typical toddler with baby fine hair, sparkling eyes, and an irresistible smile.

My wife was working for an architectural firm while I was teaching at a small liberal arts college. She took a few months off when Eddie was born and then she returned to work full time. Because my schedule was flexible, I was the one who brought Eddie to day care, picked him up after school, took him to the park and then home for dinner and a bath. He's a picky eater--toast, soup, raviolis and tomato sauce. He gets whatever he eats all over himself and we wash it off in the bath. By the time my wife arrives, at around six, Eddie's fresh and clean. She plays with him while I make our dinner. We eat and then, on alternate nights, one of us reads to Eddie, gives him a bottle of milk and puts him to bed.

This routine was fine with me, but I was not prepared for the physical closeness that comes so naturally to children. The way they like to sit on your lap or lean against you when you read to them. The way they like to hold hands when walking. The way they like to cuddle. When I was growing up, my father worked overtime and Saturdays to save money for a house and to support his wife and four kids. I don't remember his being around that much. It was my mother who stayed home with my sisters, my brother and me. She was the affectionate one.

When my father got older, he became a little sentimental--he liked an occasional hug. And my wife's father, whom I saw a few times a year, arrived and left with a bear hug. I don't feel entirely comfortable with these hugs--they feel a bit awkward. Maybe it's cultural. My father's side of the family is English and the English are famous for not showing their emotions. My mother's side is Irish. The Irish are famous for being sentimental, but even the Irish are a bit stand-offish.

Yet, I find myself hugging my son after his bath. At such times, his hair smells like freshly cut grass. He takes my face in his hands, gives me a kiss, smiles and says, "Thanks daddy." I get him dressed for bed and then we play and wrestle on the floor in his room.

I am lucky. Unlike my father, I got to feed my son, change him, read to him, bathe him, and play with him. We've been to the zoo where he's fed the animals. We ride to the playground on my bike and he goes on the swing and down the slide. Back at home I fill up his bath, he climbs in and wiggles around like an otter. At the same time, I wonder: when will the awkwardness begin? When will he draw back? When will he shun being hugged? And when will I begin to feel it is no longer appropriate to hug, embrace, kiss?

Not for a few years. I give him a horsy ride around the living room rug. (Off the rug is too painful for the knees.) We wrestle for a few minutes and tickle one another. He curls up into a ball--ticklish all over. After that it's time to read books. He picks out three. I sit on the couch and he climbs on my lap, hands me the books, makes himself comfortable and says, "Read, daddy."

SKATING

By the time my son turned five, he already had a closet full of sports equipment: a little basketball with a portable, adjustable hoop, two baseball gloves and half a dozen balls, plastic bats in various sizes, a plastic golf set, two tiny footballs, and a soccer ball. My wife and I had deliberately not given him any hockey paraphernalia. I had a friend in high school who had a scar a quarter inch thick that ran like a highway across the bridge of his nose; he had fallen in a hockey game and caught the blade of someone else's skate. I still remember Bobby Orr limping from all those knee operations, and Gordy Howe smiling, gap-toothed into the camera.

Then one Saturday in December I was at a local park with my son. He asked if we could go see the kids who were skating on the pond down the hill.

We watched kids skate by. They were younger than I'd expected. One little girl used a hockey stick to keep her balance. She kept falling and getting back up. She looked at us and smiled. A couple of teenagers flew by laughing and I suddenly remembered a Studs Terkel interview with Eric Nesterenko, a retired hockey player. Nesterenko talked about what it was he loved about hockey. It wasn't goals, assists, hat tricks, or fights; it was skating.

Even after Nesterenko had retired from hockey, he said he still liked to skate outside. I looked the interview up that day when I got home: "With the wind behind you," Nesterenko says, "you can wheel and dive and turn; you can lay yourself into impossible angles that you never could walking or running. You lay yourself at a forty-five degree angle, your elbows virtually touching the ice as you turn. Incredible!"

For Christmas I bought skates, hockey sticks and pucks for my son and me. I didn't own any skates either. The ice didn't freeze over again until the middle of January. On a Saturday morning in January, my son and I went to the pond. There was no one there. We threw sticks out onto the ice and watched them spin and slide. They made an eerie, high-pitched whine. A few big crows cawed from the tops of the pines. An old dog padded gingerly across the ice. We could have been in Maine or Canada instead of Massachusetts.

My son had on his snowsuit, wool hat and mittens. I helped him lace up his skates. Out on the ice, I held his hand and skated beside him. I turned around and skated backwards, pulling him. I let go one of his hands as he moved one foot and then the other. I let go of his other hand and held him by his collar.

"Look at me," he said.

Then he slipped and got scared so I brought him over and sat him on a bench beside the pond. I got our new hockey sticks out of the trunk of the car. I had parked behind the bench on the service road that ran through the park. He seemed happy enough on the bench, so I decided to take a run on the ice by myself. I was a little wobbly at first, but then I remembered to lean forward and push off my skates. I felt the wind against my face and I veered into a turn. The hockey stick helped me keep my balance. I crossed one skate over the other and took the turn wide. I was out over my skates. The cold wind made my eyes tear. I shook my head to clear my vision and I glided along on the top of the ice with my stick on my knees. The sky was hard and bright with a green tinge. Puffy white clouds were anchored on the horizon. I turned to skate back to where I'd left my son. Hockey stick in hand, he was up off the bench--heading for the ice.

"Wait for me," I called. I turned my skates to stop as he reached the ice, but I was going too fast, or my skates caught on something, whatever, I went flying. I flipped over on my back. He was so surprised his hands went up in the air, and he fell down on his butt. I looked over at him expecting him to be crying. Instead, he was laughing. As soon as I realized I was ok, I laughed too.

Then it hit me what caught my skate. It was his stick. Maybe hockey was his game after all. Maybe if we just got him a little plastic helmet, some gloves, elbow and knee pads, and a Bruins' jersey, it would be okay.

Hockey in the pros may seem to be about checking and power and pain, but the secret of hockey is that it has more to do with skating and having fun. Nesterenko was right. There is nothing quite like skating outside, the clean, cold winter air in your lungs, hard, bright January sun piercing the sky. With steel blades beneath your feet, you glide across the ice powered by nothing more than your own free will.

READING ALOUD

Read To Your Kids is a mantra drummed into parents today and it really seems to have sunk in. Books aimed at the young continue to be a growing market for publishers. As you know, the Harry Potter books were an international best-selling phenomenon that brought riches both to publisher and author. For parents, it is no longer enough to take books out of the library; we need to own *Goodnight Moon* and *Where the Wild Things Are* so we can read them over and over again to our enthralled children. It feels good to buy a few books for a child's birthday rather than running up the charge card with plastic toys.

In case you've been vacationing on the island of Figi for the last ten years, the reason to read books to your kids is to foster a love of reading. The idea is that if we read to them, they will be so enamored of the experience that they will go on to become great readers themselves. The subtext of the story is that this love of reading will erect an intellectual barrier of literacy that will protect the young from the evil Cyclops television. Although television does not exactly eat the young the way Cyclops ate Odysseus' men, television certainly seems to command their attention. Moreover, television stifles the imagination, which as we all know is a quiet room in the brain where a child goes when he or she reads or is read to by a loving adult.

My wife and I love to read. "A room without books is like a body without a soul," said Cicero. Our house is full of books. The idea of reading to children appeals to both of us. For our son's first twelve years in fact, (with a few exceptions) either I or my wife has read for a half hour to an hour each night to our son. We started with board books and rhyming books, fantasies and myths and nursery rhymes, from the brilliant and disturbing Maurice Sendak and the Brothers Grimm (whose cautionary tales no longer quite make sense) to the obnoxious Dr. Seuss and the benign Shel Silverstein. As our son got older, we met the ill-mannered yet entertaining Rotten Ralph, witnessed plastic cowboys and Native Americans come to life before us, and we spent a couple of weeks in a wonderful secret garden. We read all of the Oz books including a couple not so Oz written by someone other than Frank Baum. We read, reread and read again, on request, the entire *Narnia Chronicles* (all seven books) by C.S. Lewis. We slogged through Brian Jacques' violent rat adventure books. We loved getting to know Harry Potter, Huckleberry Finn and Alice.

And what was the result of these years of reading aloud? Did our son turn into a great reader? Someone who always carries d book with him just in case he had a few minutes to read while waiting in line? Someone who likes to curl up on the couch in front of the fire with a classic? Someone who asks for books for his birthday? Alack, alas, no. The result of all this reading was that our son loves to be read to. He loves to listen to books on tape when we take long trips in the car. He enjoys hearing Maureen Dowd read to him on Sunday mornings. He does not especially like to read by himself. In the summer we require that he do a little reading each day and he puts it off until he is in bed. He reads for fifteen minutes and then falls asleep. We've given him subscriptions to *Muse* and *Skateboarding* but he seems not so much to read them as to look at the photos and read the captions. He did read *Harry Potter and the Goblet of Fire,* a genuine accomplishment at 729 pages but that was because we were taking a trip to Corsica and had to spend a lot of time waiting in airports. In other words, it was a fluke.

Yes, he has succumbed to the Cyclops in the den. He prefers watching television to reading. He loves the X Games with their competitions in skateboarding, snowboarding and trick biking, all nature shows and the History channel. But he is not really discriminating. Given the chance he will watch whatever is on. After television, he reaches for skateboarding, snowboarding or car racing video games.

Was all of our reading then nothing but a waste of time? Well, no because my wife, my son and I have all enjoyed it. I hadn't even read a lot of those books. My wife had read most of them but she enjoyed reading them again. Reading aloud is an activity that brings us back to our childhood making us feel young again and brings back the pleasure of reading great books and hearing them read aloud. As many adults have discovered, there's a lot of great writing aimed at kids. Reading aloud reminds us why we like to read. Nightly reading has also become for us a family ritual. It lends structure and uniqueness to our family life. It is a family activity that we value. My son has benefited in a couple of unexpected ways too. At school he does well in English in both reading and writing, and his teachers always comment that he has a wide range of knowledge.

Until the invention of the printing press, and for a long time after that, when books were read, they were read aloud. At school and at home, entire sections of books were memorized. There is a distinct pleasure that comes from reading aloud and from hearing a well-written book read aloud. It is different from reading silently. Books like *The Great Gatsby* work better read aloud than read silently.

Lines like the following beg to be read aloud: "So we beat on, boats against the current, borne back ceaselessly into the past."

Not that we have given up on the original objective. We imagine that any day now our son will tire of video games. He will shut off the television and banish the Cyclops to the world of darkness. He will take a book down from the bookcase, lie down on the couch and begin to read. He will lose track of time so engrossed will he be. As he reaches the end of the book, he will wish it could continue. "Well," he'll say, "I can always read it again." We expect this to happen any day now.

FIFTH GRADE DANCE

It is nine p.m. on a Friday night. I'm standing on the periphery of Cunningham Hall in Milton, Massachusetts; bright lights are on overhead. The room is filled to capacity with 250 eleven-year -olds who represent the town's four elementary schools. From where I'm standing it appears that all 250 boys and girls are dancing—jumping up and down and singing along while forming the letters YMCA over their heads. They dance in groups, rather than in pairs, and seemingly, in one large masse. The energy is palpable—an electric current of positive emotion that sizzles in the air. Parents and volunteers line the walls, smiling and talking. There are no guns in the room. There have been no bomb scares. This is the news from Cunningham Hall in Milton, Massachusetts: Two hundred and fifty fifth graders dance happily to loud music while volunteers look approvingly on.

The admission ticket buys one free soda. Every child in the room appears to be healthy. No one is drinking alcohol. No one is smoking marijuana. No one is smoking crack. There are no dealers hanging outside the hall tempting the eleven-year-olds. During the two-hour dance, no one is physically abused or assaulted. There are not even any fights between the eleven-year-old boys, the eleven-year -old girls, or the adults. Boys who chase girls and girls who chase boys are told by the adults to slow down and take it easy. There are kids from the French Immersion Program and the English Program and they are dancing together. There are kids from two-family houses and kids from sprawling estates. There are white kids and black kids. There do not appear to be any racial or ethnic conflicts.

I think back to last year's dance when my son, then ten, won a dance contest. When it was announced that he had won he was surrounded by boys from his class. For a minute I thought they were going to gang up on him but no, they were clapping him on the back and shaking his hand saying, "way to go." They were not being ironic or sarcastic or in any way mean. They were happy for him.

Are there no problems at all? Beneath the surface, there are, to be sure, conflicts: social and emotional triangles. There are cliques and in-groups. During a slow dance, Chris is dancing with Leah, but Alison wants Chris to ask her to dance. Joe likes Alison and is jealous of Chris. My son likes a certain girl, but is too shy to ask her to dance. Some of these same boys who are dancing beside one another tonight have had arguments and fights at recess and after school. Not here and now.

The enthusiasm of the kids dancing infects the parents and volunteers who are all smiles. They may have problems with other adults in the room. They may disagree about school policy or whether taxes should be raised or how the library budget should be spent. They may be worried about overcrowding and lack of funding for the schools. They may want their neighbor to clean up his yard, or change the color of his house, but they seem to have forgotten or suppressed these problems for the time being.

Next year most of the children in the Hall will attend Pierce Middle School with 1000 other students. One or two years from now they will be too self-conscious to dance in a brightly lit hall surrounded by adults. They will insist that the lights be dimmed. Boys will fight with other boys over insults and over girls, and will be thrown out of dances and sent home. Girls will make fun of those girls and boys who do not dress the way they deem appropriate. Some kids will drink beer in the woods before dances and come in woozy and will be sent home or will get sick or will fight. Some kids will come to the dances high from smoking marijuana or sniffing whatever is available.

The parents and teachers who volunteer to chaperone these future dances will be tense and worried and will remain so, not just until the dance is over, but until their child's adolescence is over. But that's next year and in the years to come. The news we hear nightly on our television sets and our radios and the news we read about in the newspapers is often negative and tragic. Yet, if the news is what happens, then this too is news: 250 fifth graders got together for a town dance and had fun, dancing and sweating with the boys and girls who are their friends and who are the friends of friends in Cunningham Hall in a suburban town in the United States.

THE HELL HOUNDS

As sociologist Deborah Tannen points out, men are big on one-upmanship. I ran into this recently when I was talking to a male colleague. I told him I had to leave a meeting to run a soccer practice.

"How's your team doing?" he asked.

"Not so great," I said laughing. "We're in last place."

"I coach in Norton," he said smiling. "We're in first."

I just nodded. He had one-upped me. That was okay though because I was trying my hardest, doing my best, right? So, my soccer team was not number one—big deal. Well, actually, my team, the Hell Hounds, as they named themselves, had not won one game.

I've coached soccer, basketball, and baseball in town leagues for a number of years. Most of my teams won more than they lost. Not this team. This season the other teams in our division (11 and 12-year -ld boys) seemed bigger, older, more mature. My guys were small and fragile. One collision with an opponent, or even with the ball, seemed to traumatize them. They'd fall down and wouldn't get up until the referee blew his whistle and all the players on the field went down on one knee. When my guys did regain their feet, they'd stagger to the sidelines holding their tummies, or they'd limp across the field on the verge of tears. I'd give them a pat on the back and tell them they'd be okay. I also had a couple of wide bodies who did not move very much. This is more of a problem in soccer than it might be in say, football. I did have three, maybe four good players, but they were not quite good enough to take over a game; there were no Mia's or Beckem's on the team.

As a result, my good players felt as if they could not depend on their teammates and tried to do it all themselves. We did score now and then. In fact, we were tied at the end of the first half in a number of games, but then we'd get creamed in the second half. The good players would get tired and when I subbed for them, the other team would score. One of my back-ups always went the wrong way; he'd trip his own teammates, steal the ball and kick it out of bounds. He told me he got so nervous he couldn't focus. I nodded in an understanding way.

My team was not in great shape. Video games may be fun but aren't great for the legs or the wind. I told myself all they needed was practice. I held practices after school. Three players would show. I'd play to even out the teams. It's a big field when you play soccer two on two.

One week my son, who happened to be our best defenseman, said after the game that he didn't want to play anymore. I knew exactly how he felt. I didn't want to coach anymore. In fact, I had not signed up to coach. I thought I needed a little break from coaching so I signed my son up for the league and wrote right on the form that I was not interested in coaching. A week before the season was to begin, I received a team roster and a notice that I was to pick up uniforms for team number 5, Division 48, the following weekend. I called up the Coordinator of the Division to complain. "We had to draft people to coach," she said. "Hardly anyone volunteered."

"I thought volunteerism was up in America," I said.

"Not in this league," she quipped.

We tell our kids that it doesn't matter whether they win or lose as long as they do their best. We tell them to remember that they are playing for fun, but it isn't much fun when you lose every game. It's depressing. Does it build character? I don't know. I suppose it teaches us that when we make a commitment to do something that we have to follow through and honor our commitment, even when we didn't really sign up to coach. But I have mixed feelings about it. One day I called off practice because it was kind of cold out.

The last game I implored them to do their best and have fun. I told them this would be the game they would win. "Play like a team, make the pass, focus, play hard the whole game." I patted them on the back and yelled encouragement from the sidelines. The final score was 1-1.

"Both teams won!" I exclaimed. I urged them not to be discouraged and wished them better luck next year. Our final record for the season was 0-9-1.

We Americans are a hardy crew. That first winter in 1620 was tough but we hung on. Later, in King Philip's War, our numbers were cut in half; we were pushed back to the sea, but we survived. We know that work is our salvation. But we also know it isn't enough to try hard and do your best. Sometimes you need to win.

PLAYING HARDBALL

The writer Min-zhan Lu says, "Teach them from the beginning to struggle." She is speaking of education where, she says, children must struggle in order to learn. We don't often think of sports from this angle. We may think of sports as a healthy way to be aggressive, or as a good forum for socializing and making friends. We may see sports as a place where kids learn the value of teamwork, develop self-discipline, and stay out of trouble, but sports are also fields of struggle where kids learn to deal with the fear of failure, and the fear of getting hurt.

I've coached and managed a Little League baseball team for the past five years. My son and his friends have been on my team since they were five. Last year, at the age of nine, they pitched from a Little League mound. They hit live pitching and they played, for the first time, with official hardballs. Fortunately, there was only one serious injury--trying to catch a fly ball, a left fielder on another team fractured a bone just beneath his eye. Catching, pitching and hitting hardballs, the nine-year-olds began to get an inkling of the seriousness we attach to games in America.

I've been working with my son for about six years now--playing catch, throwing him grounders and pop-ups, giving him hitting practice and catching his pitching, showing him what I know about form and grip, stance, balance and focus. Last year, our team lost a few good players and picked up a few who hadn't played much. For the first time since I began coaching, we lost more than we won. I felt sorry for my son one game in particular when he was having a tough outing on the mound. He couldn't seem to get it over. After he had one out, he walked three kids in a row. He kicked the dirt and talked to himself. His poor pitching affected his usually excellent fielding too. A couple of routine grounders turned into errors on bad throws to first and the other team scored twice. I might have taken him out but really there was no one else on the team who would do any better. So, I left him in to struggle and work his way out of it. He walked in another run but then someone hit a fly ball. Our second baseman caught it and tagged out a runner who was off second. Sometimes your teammates pick you up.

It was a season in which the nine-year-olds learned what occurs when you don't get your glove up in front of your face on a fly ball and what happens when you don't jump out of the way of an inside pitch. In one at-bat, our right fielder, Tony, was hit square in the back by a fastball. He never saw it coming. He was staring at the ground, hoping for a walk. We had a terrific catcher, Danny, who would jump out of the batter's box at every pitch because he was hit in the helmet once early in the season. He learned what it's like to be called out on strikes and to swing wildly at balls he had no chance on. Patrick discovered what it's like to hit the ball hard with the barrel of the bat and watch it fly over the fence, and Joey learned how it feels to slide under a tag at home plate. If they didn't know it already, they learned that coaches sometimes make mistakes and that umpires make bad calls.

Even though they were only nine, they already had ideas about themselves and their teammates as ballplayers. They were convinced that they weren't very good at pitching or that they were. They thought that they couldn't hit for beans or that they were sluggers. They talked about who knew how to catch and who didn't. Of course, they all improved during the spring, and if they stick with baseball, their skills will change and develop. Yet, by the end of last season, Danny and Joey had already decided they had had enough of baseball. They said they'd concentrate on hockey. It was also true that only a few of our players seemed to try to do their best. You could see who wanted to win—and who was willing to listen and to learn.

As a coach, the struggle lies between wanting to give kids every chance to play and wanting to give the team the best chance of winning. Parents of the players complicate those decisions. One parent kept asking me to put his son in to pitch. Finally, in a game in which we were down by five runs in the sixth, I figured Why not? I put Zack in. When he tried to pitch, he couldn't reach the plate. He walked the first batter he faced with four pitches. "You can do it, Zack," yelled his father from the stands. Then Zack began crying. He dropped the ball and walked off the mound to the bench. And whose fault was that? Mine, of course.

Parents of the players can be a problem in Little League. I remember coaching a game of five-year-olds. When a batter was thrown out at first, he cried. His mother asked if he could just stay on the base. When I said, "No, sorry." I felt like a villain. At the end of the game, a number of parents told their kids they hadn't lost even though the game wasn't even close.. "It was a tie," they said.

Each season, as a coach, you want to put kids in the positions that will help the team and that doesn't always fit the expectations of their parents. You can't make everyone happy. One of the things parents seem to forget is that these coaching positions are voluntary. Little League is really an amazing phenomenon when you think about it. All these people, fathers mostly, dedicating their time to coaching young kids.

Sports can be where kids learn how it feels to win. They may also learn that if they work hard, practice and focus, they may do well, but they may not always win. In this respect, sports are like many other activities in which kids learn who they are and what they are capable of. They learn how to deal with struggle, to work their way out of a slump or a jam. Struggle, as players and later in life, as coaches, is something we all have to learn to deal with.

HONDURAS, 2018

Each morning we'd board a yellow school bus and pass through the polluted, crowded, traffic-jammed streets of the capital of Honduras, Tegucigalpa, where police and security guards armed with pump shotguns and automatic weapons stood in weary pairs at each corner. We'd drive for an hour into the mountains where horses and burros paid no attention to truck drivers passing each other on blind curves. We'd arrive at the San Isidro Church to labor with a dozen Honduran men and women and their children.

Our group consisted of three men, five women and two sixteen-year-old boys. Jenny, fluent in Spanish, was the most valuable member of the group. She was the conduit between the skilled construction crew and us; she would tell us what they wanted us to do. We were helping construct a concrete courtyard, walled garden and steps. The boys, Joe and Eddie, might tie off metal rods for a rebar. Their mothers, Kate and Elizabeth, could carry water from a cistern to the concrete mixer. James, Bernhard and I would jump in where needed, shoveling sand and rocks to make concrete, filling wheelbarrows, troweling cement smooth. Elizabeth and Kate would make lunches for the workers and us. Jenny always seemed to find time to play with the Honduran children who drifted in from the surrounding houses. The six members of the Honduran construction crew were paid eight dollars a day. There were also a few local farmers and their wives and teenage sons, members of the church, who worked, like us, as volunteers.

That Saturday, we visited Jocomico, a remote mountain village where 32 children sat, neatly dressed, in a one room school, surrounded by tin and cardboard walls with branches supporting a tin roof. Boards on tree stumps provided seats and long wooden planks served as desks. A handful of books were shared by the class. The teacher used a small chalkboard mounted on a stand for lessons. We listened to the children, aged 5-14, sing Spanish songs with gusto. They answered, smiling, in unison, an enthusiastic Si! when asked if they liked school. The teacher was a Honduran law student who was being paid a stipend by the government. Each morning, he took the bus from Tegucigalpa and walked the three-mile path from the road to the school.

The Christ Church, that's our church, was funding the building of a one-room, cement block schoolhouse in Jocomico, as well as providing school supplies for the students.

That day, we helped clear the land around what would be the new schoolhouse, stacked cinder blocks for the construction crew and carried rocks through the mud to lay a foundation for the new building.

The next afternoon, back at San Isidro, the Pastor introduced us to Mother Toyo (mother of all), the 81-year-old matriarch of the community. She formally welcomed us and thanked us for coming. "You are sending a good message by doing the work you are doing, a good message to those who live here and in the surrounding communities."

As Eliot said, the people of Honduras are "not known, not looked for." Perhaps we went there in part, to know them, and to represent the Christ Church and all those members of the wider community who supported the mission with funds and supplies. But I also think our mission was to offer an alternative view of what America is and who Americans are. When I asked a couple of Honduran co-workers at San Isidro, 14-year-old Juan Ramon and his father Hugo, if they liked the United States, they said without hesitation, "Yes." "Why?" I asked. "Because of the people," they said.

THE ALLIANCE

Five Skidmore students, two males and three females, stood in the road in front of us wearing nothing but their birthday suits and sneakers. It was Fun Day at Skidmore. My son, Eddie, was driving me, my wife and his girlfriend, Ramsey, back to his dorm from dinner in Saratoga Springs. My wife and I had come up from Boston for a quick last visit before graduation. Saratoga is beautiful in the spring, and we wanted to begin trekking home some of the clutter our son had accumulated over four years. When we spotted the nude coeds, Eddie told us that it was a tradition at Skidmore for students to run naked across campus on Fun Day. Right around then, one of the girls in the group spotted my son driving our car and yelled out: "Eddie!"

With a great shout, the nudist mob charged us. Eddie stopped the car and they climbed onto the hood and reached in the windows. I was riding in the front trying not to stare between my crossed hands at the perfect body of a twenty-one-year-old girl.

"Noooo!" cried Eddie. "These are my parents!"

Glancing over I could see he was really embarrassed. Meanwhile, my wife and I were laughing. The girls in the SI Swimsuit edition wearing next to nothing may be erotic, but five nude coeds in running shoes are ridiculous. I suddenly got an image from thirty years before of playing nude waffle ball on a beach on Martha's Vineyard. It reminded me of something else too, but I couldn't put my finger on it. The primordial clan climbed off the car and Eddie drove on to his dorm.

Two weeks later, my wife and I drove down for graduation. That night, we had dinner out with my wife's sister and brother, along with Ramsey's mom, dad and her grandmother. After dinner Eddie told us that his band, Gung Ho, was getting together for one last set at their dorm and we were invited. We all decided to go and when we got there, crowded in the dorm common room and hanging out back were the parents, brothers and sisters, aunts and uncles and a few grandparents of the members of the band. Also hanging outside were about thirty students. Some looked familiar.

Most of the parents had already heard the band's songs. Some of us sang along to "Another Shot of Whiskey." All of us there, that night, this mix of generations and ages, it suddenly just felt so different from my generation's experience with our parents. It reminded me of something else too—that's what I'd been trying to think of before--a feeling of shared experience that my generation knew for a short time in the late sixties and early seventies.

I thought of listening to campus bands jam afternoons in 1970 at the pond at UMass-Amherst. We'd boogie in groups and sometimes when it was warm out, women would take off their tops while dancing. For a few years my generation felt united by music and we have that connection with our kids who grew up listening to rock and roll. Rock contains within it a Dionysian element of wildness and rebellion. That musical link helps create a sense of community between boomers and millennials.

Then I thought back to all those conflicts I grew up with: fights over long hair and music and independence and women's rights and race relations and Vietnam and censorship and of course, sex. Boomers and the "silent" generation were like rams butting heads and locking horns.

In the coming years there will be generational conflicts over Social Security and Medicare. Young people may get tired of paying for baby boomers who refuse to die, but for now, baby boomers and millennials still seem to be getting along pretty well. They may be tribal with their tattoos, text-speak and Facebook friends, but they seem happy to hang out with the elders now and then. Maybe because we have a few experiences in common, among them: wild parties, skinny dipping, and rock music.

My son is moving from Boston to New York City next month to live in a loft with his band and look for day jobs and nighttime gigs. I'll miss him. But any time I want to retrieve that feeling of shared experience I had standing outside his dorm, I just play Gung Ho and sing along.

FINE FEATHERED FRIENDS

When I moved with my family to a house just outside of town, one of my first purchases was a wooden birdfeeder. I had always liked birds and thought it would be nice to gaze out the window and watch them feed while I was standing at the counter cutting up vegetables for salad or preparing dinner. Oh yes, I was naïve, clueless, a babe in the urban woods. I didn't know then that squirrels operate a ground to tree network where nothing happens without their approval. Above the ground, in the trees and in the air, crows rule. They've unionized and all other birds must get their permission to nest or feed. Crows do not go in for birdseed but are after bigger game. They line telephone wires waiting for road-kill and search backyards for eggs in the nests of the smaller birds, all of whom are at their mercy.

The squirrels made a mockery of my early efforts. One sat on the squirrel-proof feeder that was suspended from an elm in the middle of the back yard pressing a lever with his foot releasing birdseed to be collected by his friend on the ground below. Another member of the gang squatted on his haunches on our cedar picnic bench munching on sunflower seeds and spitting out the shells onto the grass. I went through a series of feeders, all guaranteed to be safe from squirrels, until I realized that there aren't any feeders safe from squirrels. Instead, I decided to find places to hang the feeders that the squirrels couldn't get to.

I tried a number of different trees, using both wire and rope to suspend the feeders but the squirrels danced on the branches like tightrope artists. Half a dozen of them were now running a small circus between my yard and my neighbor's. They chattered all morning and chased each other between feedings for fun. I hung one feeder outside a kitchen window. It was safe from squirrels, but the white and black splotches of bird remains proved unappetizing as did the sound of birds thwacking against the glass because they failed to see the window. I finally settled on hanging a couple of feeders from the support beams just beneath the roof of the garage.

At first all went well. The wild birdseed I was using drew a beautiful northern cardinal. A hairy woodpecker set up shop in an old maple tapping his name in Morse code on the trunk. A mocking bird worked out his daily identity crises from the apex of the roof of the garage. Starlings foraged for seed on the lawn. Crows dropped down to dig up grubs and robins searched for worms. A couple of mourning doves appeared every afternoon and cooed the early evening in. Once or twice a chickadee or a goldfinch stopped by.

But then, I don't know, maybe it was the crows tipping off the other birds. Crows are very social and actually love to share if there is enough to go around, or maybe the birds were just being curious and following the crowd that began to show up. Whatever, I walked out one morning to find my yard had become the site of a neighborhood block party for birds. My back-yard feeders were a buffet with "All you can Eat" written all over them. It was like Rockefeller Center at Christmas. Fourth of July! Woodstock! There must have been 200 sparrows on the roof of the garage waiting to get at the feeders. A nervy crowd too, pushing and shoving one another off the gutter. There was a gang of big gray pigeons on the grass picking up the remains tossed to them by a dozen chunky squirrels. When the squirrels weren't eating, they were sharpening their teeth on the legs of our picnic bench which looked as if it had been attacked by beavers. Up in the trees a battery of crows squawked and cawed so I couldn't hear myself think.

What could I do? Call the police and have them all arrested? Ask the fire department to give them a good hosing down? Borrow my son's paintball gun and teach them all a good lesson? I decided to wait them out.

When the seed was all gone, and it didn't take long, they left in search of another party. Talk about fair weather friends! Well, that was the end of the daily feedings. Now I only invite all the animals in the neighborhood to Sunday Brunch. The rest of the week, they're on their own.

THE PET REPUBLIC

A few months ago, my wife and I brought a puppy into our empty nest to give us someone to talk to and take walks with. Mookie (named after baseball great Mookie Betts) has been fun but demanding. Whenever visitors came over, he'd bark like crazy and he had a tendency to claw holes in my go-to jeans and bite into the sleeves of my sweatshirts. My wife and I had to wear shoes in the house because he attacked our bare feet.

We decided we had to enroll Mookie in puppy kindergarten. We live in Somerville, near the Cambridge line, just outside Boston. Just down the street from us, on Mass. Ave. is The Pet Republic. Cambridge is well known as a bastion of p.c. They have a weekly mulch pick-up. They have outlawed plastic bags in stores. And Cambridge is the home of Harvard and MIT. The other day I was walking past MIT when I spotted a group of students sitting cross-legged in an area taped off and designated as a "judgment-free zone." Not that there's anything wrong with that!

So, I should not have been surprised when I found out that the training is all about positive reinforcement at The Pet Republic. "We don't use negative tactics," Hannah, our instructor, said to me. "We use treats and shower them with praise," she said smiling.

"What if Mookie is biting my ankle?" I asked.

"Just make like a tree and ignore him," she said. "He'll soon stop."

Hannah not only works at The Pet Republic she is also a trainer at the Aquarium where she teaches manners to seals. Hannah is very upbeat and obviously loves animals.

She sometimes reminded me of a dolphin the way she chirped and hopped about the room when working with pets. So, I can't really question her knowledge of the animal world, but I began to wonder whether we didn't need a little more than just praise to curb Mookie's bad habits. He was chewing into the chairs in the living room and tearing magazines to shreds. No one wanted to visit us anymore.

We may have hit on the right balance with an outfit called Zen Dog Training. There, they use mostly positive reinforcement but when it comes to objectionable behavior, they redirect the dog to another activity and, if necessary, they even use the N word—that's the word No. They told us to put the puppy in time-out if necessary. This is apparently a version of removing him from the pack--something puppies really hate.

According to Zen Dog, we were falling into the same trap that many of today's parents fall into. We were spoiling our puppy! We were letting him run the household and take over our lives. As a result, like the kids of parents who give their children whatever they want and lavish them with praise, Mookie would act out jealously with guests and take advantage of our good graces whenever he could. If we didn't correct him now, he would grow up to be a boomer! As you can see, we have our work cut out for us, but we are up for the challenge and if we fail, there is always pet therapy.

BITTERSWEET VACATION

My wife and I bought a place a few years ago in Wellfleet—a beautiful spot on the outer banks of Cape Cod. We thought it would be great for family vacations. But after graduating from college, my son moved with his roommates to Brooklyn. Brooklyn is a Mecca for millennials. There are plenty of jobs and even more ways to spend the money at night. But it isn't easy to get from Brooklyn to the outer banks of the Cape.

Eddie and his girlfriend Gabby take the train from Brooklyn to Manhattan where they catch a bus to Boston. From Boston they take a ferry to Provincetown where my wife and I pick them up and drive them back to Wellfleet. This summer, because of other commitments to weddings and events with friends, they were only able to take four days off to come stay with us. The trip here takes most of the first day. Not long after they settle in, we have some burgers on the grill, corn and salad with tomatoes and cucumbers from my garden. We catch up on news after dinner and then they're ready for bed.

Last summer the weather was spectacular—sunny, 75-85 degrees, not too humid, and some days surprisingly cool. Although it was in the low 70s that Saturday, we headed to the beach. We're a couple of miles away from White Crest—one of the most beautiful beaches in the U.S. with 50-foot sand dunes, white crystalline sand, and 2-4 foot waves--perfect for swimming and surfing. We bring horseshoes, a football, a plastic bat and a whiffle ball. There's plenty of room at White Crest for games. The crowds go to the beach a mile away where the bar sits on top of the dunes.

Horseshoes goes back a couple of thousand years to when people first started shoeing horses. Peasants made up the game with discarded horseshoes. It's a great beach game. You push the stakes into the sand about 40 feet apart. You need to keep your eye on your throws because the shoes can sink like anchors into the sand and disappear. Eddie and his girlfriend Gabby play against my wife and me and by the time the game is over, we're ready to dive in for a dip. By August the water is just about 60 degrees—warm for New England. Gabby points out grey seals just offshore.

After we swim, we throw the football around for a while and then set up a game of whiffle ball. We use towels for bases. The score is close for a few innings but it turns out that Gabby has a killer curve and my son hits a home run to win. There was time when I could outhit him but that time is long gone.

When the game is over, we pack up and head to one of the ponds—kettle ponds they call them, formed when the glaciers retreated 12,000 years ago. The water is so clear you can see the bottom if you look down as you swim, and of course, the water in the pond is much warmer than the ocean.

After that it's back to the house for outdoor showers, margaritas, and grilled swordfish for dinner outside on the deck. Gabby, who is a lawyer, is passionate about a sexual harassment case she's working on, and Eddie is enthusiastic about a 3D printing project. The next day is cloudy so we go for a long bike ride along the harbor and up Old Chequessett Road to Truro. That night we go out for lobster rolls. It's awesome all right, but there's a bittersweet feeling in the air.

The next day my wife and I drop them at the ferry so they can make their long trek back to Brooklyn. It's a beautiful breezy day. The streets of Provincetown are jammed. There always seems to be a festival of one kind or another there.

They wish they could stay longer. We wish they could stay longer. The ferry is loading at the end of the dock. Will there ever be a summer when there's enough time?

WHAT I LEARNED
IN SIXTH GRADE

By the time fifth grade rolled around, my family had moved four times since I'd started elementary school. Three of these moves were in the same working-class city just south of Boston: Quincy. Each move meant a new school and by the time I arrived at the fourth school, I had a social survival plan all worked out. It was simple: on the first day of school, I picked a fight. I knew that win or lose I would immediately make friends. I chose a cocky Irish kid named Jimmy Donovan. He was about my size so it seemed fair. I was soon sitting on his chest telling him to give when a teacher pulled me off. Sure enough, that afternoon after school, half a dozen kids walked me home and told me I was welcome in their gang.

It turned out they were the ones who ruled the school. The group's leader, Larry Bray, had been kept back the year before and he was the toughest kid in school. I was pretty happy with myself until about two weeks later when Jimmy Donovan sucker punched me in gym class. I beat him up again but no matter how many times I hit him, he would not give up. He was like one of those blow-up clowns that bounce back when you push them down. When I asked him why he wouldn't relent, he said, "Us Donovans never quit!" After that we fought regularly, whenever we were left alone together. The school put us in different classes, and by sixth-grade graduation, both of us were told to stay home. But I've gotten ahead of myself.

I remained convinced I'd made the right move because I was a member in good standing of Larry's gang, but then, in sixth grade, Larry's right hand man Al decided we should form a woman-hater's club. This seemed like a fine idea at the time since we constantly complained about girls. They were all good students, they dressed up for school, they had better manners that we did and they were more mature. We had a right to be angry. We were also beginning to go through puberty and so were finding ourselves attracted to those girls. The club was a good way to deny this.

Meanwhile, America was changing its attitude toward sex. Chubby Checker was twisting the night away and Elvis was grinding his hips on television. Elizabeth Taylor was burning up the big screen with Peter Newman.

I developed a secret crush on a girl in my class, Judy Taylor. I had been a little leery of women since second grade when Janie invited me to her house for milk and cookies. There was no one home and after our snack as I stood up to go, she pulled me toward her, kissed me and then pushed me down, ran into her room and shut the door. I fell and hit my head on the radiator. I wandered home in a daze and decided not to trust girls from then on. But four years later I was swooning over Judy Taylor's long black hair and violet eyes. I gave her a note in English asking her if she'd like to go the Carnival that was parked behind the high school that weekend.

It was the perfect date. We went on the rides together and walked around holding hands. At the shooting concession I won her a fake silver bracelet. I didn't see anyone else there from school but Monday morning Al confronted me. "We heard you gave Judy Taylor a bracelet," he said.

"No way, I would never..." I shook my head and looked away.

The next weekend I took Judy to see an Elvis matinee at the Wollaston Theater. We kissed near the end of the movie and walked out of the theater holding hands.

Al and Larry were waiting outside and Al punched me in the stomach just as I emerged into the sunlight.

"Liar!" he yelled and he and Larry ran off laughing.

I was officially out of the gang.

I soon made friends with a nicer group of kids who seldom fought and were not women- haters. About a month later a girl picked a fight with Al in the school playground. Al hit her in the chest and knocked her out. That afternoon we called a meeting of all sixth-grade boys after school. Larry laid down the law. No more hitting girls. The woman-haters club was disbanded. Larry and Al and I nodded at each other. We weren't friends exactly but we were no longer enemies.

And when my family moved the summer after sixth grade to the middle-class town of Milton and I had to start at a new school, I did not pick a fight with someone.

FIRST YEAR

I met Joyce at an orientation party and we started hanging out after that. She was quiet like me. She had sad dark eyes and long auburn hair. She reminded me of Natalie Wood. I was a rebel without a cause rescuing her from boredom. Surprisingly, she was not self-confident despite being so pretty and she didn't seem to believe me when I complimented her.

"You look beautiful tonight," I'd say. And she'd go, "Really?"

Neither of us had much sexual experience. I'd slept with one other girl the summer before almost to get it over with when I had visited a friend who had a house on Cape Cod. We'd been good friends all through high school and when we had sex, we both agreed right after that it just didn't feel right and we wanted to remain friends. Joyce told me her first was her prom date.

UMass-Amherst was a shock for a lot of us coming from the suburbs. It was huge with 20,000 students and a big campus that felt like a city. I was happy to hook up early with Joyce. I had tried out for the football team. I was a pretty good fullback and linebacker in high school but at UMass, the players were much bigger and stronger. I lasted two weeks. I got a concussion running back a kick-off in practice and a couple of days later, turned in my uniform. I'd already had two concussions in high school and even then, I knew they were not good for the brain.

Joyce and I would meet on a Friday night, drop by one of the five thousand parties on campus for a few beers and then head back to her dorm. She liked to get high so I always brought a joint and got in the habit of carrying one in my wallet. Something that would come back to haunt me a couple of years later when I was arrested for drinking and disturbing the peace. This was after the college turned against us because of the strike in 1970. From then on, the Amherst police would come on campus and haul us in for being rowdy. At the police station, the cops found a joint in my wallet and added possession to the charges.

So, that fall, 1969, Joyce and I would throw a record on the turntable: Linda Ronstadt or James Taylor or the Beach Boys, and we'd smoke a joint. She'd lucked into a single room when her roommate dropped out in the first week. Quite a few kids dropped out. I ran into the President of my high school class early on and he said to me, "This place is a zoo! I'm out of here." He left that week.

Joyce and I took it kind of slow. We'd turn off the lights, get undressed, (she was shy though she had a great body). In the dark I'd slip on a condom and we'd have intercourse. I tried to do make sure she enjoyed it though I didn't really know what I was doing.

I was an English major and Joyce was in the Business Program. I had a great Composition professor who liked my writing and recommended books to me. Joyce hated her classes. She said she was only taking Business because that's what her parents wanted.

One night near the end of the semester we were walking back from a party when we ran across a couple of dudes fighting. I knew one of them. He was a tackle on the football team. He was way bigger than the other kid whom I didn't know. "Hardy!" I said, that was the big guy's last name, "Lay off that kid." I thought he'd remember me but he was pretty drunk.

He turned and charged me. Next thing I knew there's this 250-pound dude swinging at me. I got in a couple of shots, but he tackled me and I fell backward down some steps. We were on a plaza. I hit my head and blacked out.

Next thing I knew Joyce was leaning over me asking me if I was all right. I was groggy but I got up and Joyce helped me get to the infirmary where the doctor gave me stitches for the split lip Hardy left me. Plus, my nose was swollen and my head hurt.

I took a couple of days off and the semester ended and I headed back to my parents' house in Quincy to recover. I was surprised I didn't hear from Joyce over the break. I called her house a couple of times (she lived about an hour away in Worcester). A woman told me Joyce wasn't available. Joyce had warned me that her parents were protective so I just figured we'd talk when we returned to school.

Back at UMass, Joyce's room was empty. The dorm counselor said she wasn't coming back. I tried calling her house again. This time her father answered and told me that Joyce was taking the semester off and didn't want to hear from me. I didn't know what to think of that. I wondered if she dumped me because of the fight. Maybe it scared her; I did look like a horror show that night. Anyway, I couldn't figure it out. It was like when Natalie Wood was kidnapped by the Comanches in *The Searchers*. I should have pulled a John Wayne and rescued her but I wasn't sure she wanted to be rescued.

Meanwhile, things were heating up on campus. We'd had a visit from Hubert Humphrey who had lost to Nixon in 1968 and all of us Democrats kind of blamed him. He gave a speech in the gym and at the end, students heckled him about the war in Vietnam. Humphrey called out: "Why don't you just go to the Pub and get drunk if you're going to act like that!" It didn't go over too well, and it riled the campus up. Everyone started arguing about politics, Nixon, Vietnam, the bombings.

In the spring members of the Weathermen, a radical group, showed up on campus and took over the school newspaper writing articles about protests and the military industrial complex. Everyone started skipping classes and taking drugs. We'd gather at the campus pond and groove to boogie music. James Montgomery's Blues band would jam.

We had workshops and marches through Amherst. Someone threw a brick through a big bank window downtown. I found a new group of friends who did drugs and were into politics and that May, after the Kent State shootings, five of us drove down to DC for the demonstrations. I don't actually remember too much about it. We were high the entire weekend. I remember hearing Joni Mitchell and marching and sleeping on top of the hood of the car. Then we drove back to school.

The campus had been shut down. No one would be penalized for demonstrating or missing class. We packed up and headed home for the summer early. Yup, we had won. Closed down the school and Nixon was promising to bring home the troops. Everything was going to change. America would become a peaceful country. Our generation was going to make America into a big happy utopian community. I went home to work construction for the summer and hang out with my high school friends.

Well, I returned in the fall and school was back to normal as if the protests had never happened. The atmosphere was a little different though. The campus police weren't so friendly with us. Word spread around that we had to be careful at parties. Arrests would be made.

Late that September I ran into Joyce. "Hey, what happened to you?" I asked.

"Let's get a coffee," she said. She still looked great to me and the months we'd spent together came rushing back.

"I'm sorry I couldn't talk to you last spring," she said. "When I got home, my parents found a joint in my room and had me committed to McLean's. They're really conservative and strict."

"McLean's hospital? Why would they do that?"

She sipped her coffee. "I made the mistake of telling my mother that we were sleeping together and that I was afraid I might be pregnant."

"That's crazy," I said and immediately regretted it. "I mean, I always used a condom."

She put down her coffee. "Wait, what?" she looked down at the table. "Really?"

"You didn't know?"

"No," she said. "No, I didn't know. In fact, emotionally, I was kind of a mess."

"I guess I should have told you, but I assumed you did know. I'm really sorry. How long were you at McClean's?"

"Three months," she said.

"Jesus, that's unbelievable."

"Borderline schizophrenia was the diagnosis," she said. She had a weary look that made her seem older.

"The joint was one you got from me, right?"

She nodded.

"Wow, I feel terrible," I took her hand. "Can I see you?" I asked.

She stood up. "I don't think so," she said. "I just think I better get my shit together. Focus on school. Maybe in a few months."

I sat there and thought about what happened. If I had known what she was going through, I would have driven out to her house and at least tried to rescue her. Instead, I was like Robert Wagner, Natalie's husband who let her fall off the boat after she'd had a few drinks and he didn't even go in and try to prevent her from drowning.

I just sat there and watched Joyce walk right out of my life. UMass was a big school. I never saw her again.

TOO MUCH DRAMA

I was happy I did not find her attractive. She was a blue-eyed blond with a big smile, a little chunky, not fat but she could lose a few pounds. Those days I went for the more exotic type—black hair, dark eyes—the opposite of all the girls in my Irish/English family.

My roommate Will and I were picking her up at the train station in Banff. We were in the final year of a graduate writing program at University of Montana. Will and I got together because a New York Jew and an Irish Catholic from Boston had more in common with each other than either of us had with the aspiring writers from Montana and Colorado and Utah who populated the MFA Program at University of Montana in 1975. Will and I both liked Bruce Springsteen and we had the same self-deprecating, sardonic sense of humor. Neither of us could believe that we were surrounded by actual cowboys and native Americans. Will was a good friend to me almost right away. He had a Mustang he let me use and he was always bringing home an extra six-pack of Olympia beer or a couple of steaks to grill.

We picked up Kate that day in September and drove south through the Rockies to the panhandle of Idaho and back to Missoula, Montana. Will and I had rented a house in town. There were two bedrooms but the walls were thin and I usually kept my door open at night to keep the air flowing. Some nights I'd watch Kate sail past on her way to the bathroom in white panties after they'd had sex. Once she got settled in and cleaned up, I had to admit she was more attractive than I had first thought she was. Her smile was warm and friendly and her eyes had a mischievous cast that made you think she was in on something funny. Her voice was low with a softness to it, almost a purr. She was enthusiastic about little things like the taste of fresh bread or the way coriander accented chili. Because Will and I had slightly different schedules, I would sometimes find myself home alone with her.

That fall, she started talking to me about how she wasn't sure she'd made the right decision coming out and joining Will. They'd gotten together senior year at William and Mary. After graduating, she moved back home to Buffalo and Will went to the Creative Writing Program at U of Montana. When Will invited her out to Montana, she took him up on the offer because she was living with her parents and going nowhere career-wise. She thought Montana was worth a try but after about a month she was starting to feel she had made a mistake. She wanted advice on how to tell Will. Meanwhile, she had picked up a job at a local restaurant and had decided to stay in the area whatever happened.

I started missing a class now and then to hang out with her. She was so open with me, I felt as if I had known her for years. One day we were there by ourselves cleaning up. I was carrying a dish to the sink and she turned into me and we stared at each other. We were just a few inches apart. Her mouth was probably her best feature. She had thick, full lips and when she wasn't smiling, they had temptation written all over them. Then there was that velvety voice. She went on to do voice-over years later and I still hear her voice sometimes at the beginnings and end of programs. So, I kissed her. I felt one of those instant connections you feel only a few times in your life. I was pulled in by the way she smelled and by the hue and texture of her skin. We spent the afternoon in bed.

Edith Wharton had a theory that love must be forbidden to be worthwhile. In the movie version of Wharton's novel *The Age of Innocence,* Jeremy Irons only loves Michelle Peiffer when he is engaged to someone else. Years later when his wife dies and he has the chance to get together with the woman he has loved for twenty years, he passes it up—it would be too much of a letdown. Wharton was onto something. The intensity comes in part from the risk, the breaking of the rules.

We were surreptitious for a couple of weeks before we finally confronted Will and confessed. He did not take it well. He was very emotional about it. Said he was losing both his best friend and the love of his life. I felt awful but she was in the process of breaking up with him anyway, right? Meanwhile, we had fallen for each other. Isn't that the expression? You <u>fall</u> in love? Like it's not in your control, it just happens...

Winter lasts a good six months in Montana. Slate gray skies and snow drifts and relentless cold. Kate packed her things and took a bus to Seattle. Will remained in the house with me but the keys to the car were no longer left on the kitchen table, and I had to buy my own beer and food. We no longer ate together. We were civil but we weren't friends.

Kate picked up a job as a waitress in Seattle and stayed with some friends of her parents until she found her own apartment. In the spring I hitched out to see her every couple of weeks. In between visits we wrote letters. We were completely open with each other. When she slept with someone in Seattle she told me about it. If I went home with a woman in the MFA Program I told Kate.

When I graduated from University of Montana, Kate and I went back East to live and work on an apple orchid in

New Hampshire. Kate's sister's boyfriend had a connection with the owner. We lived in a tent during the entire harvest. I loved it but Kate soon got sick of grading apples and going without showers for days.

We moved down to Boston, and found an apartment in the North End. I got a job as a bartender (I'd worked as a bartender in college) and I convinced my boss to hire Kate as a waitress. This was in the disco era and it was a high-volume nightclub where Evelyn Champagne King and the Tramps played. Quite a change from the apple orchid. It wasn't what we wanted to do for a living but I figured we would find permanent jobs eventually. I had already decided I wanted to marry Kate. I was just waiting for the right moment to pop the question.

One night it was a little slow at the club and the boss told Kate and a couple of the bartenders they could go home. Tony and Vinny and Kate sat at my bar and had a few free drinks and Tony said he'd be happy to drop her off. I remember watching her walk out with the two guys thinking, *Ought oh*. Tony always had drugs he dealt on the side: cocaine, Percocet, speed.

I didn't get home until a couple of hours later. We were having sex when she started crying. She told me Tony had offered her a couple of downs. She took them and the combination with the drinks sent her over the edge. The next thing she knew, Vinny was banging her in the back seat of Tony's Cadillac. Then Tony took his place. She said he couldn't really get it up.

I wanted to be sympathetic. I realized it wasn't completely her fault. But she didn't have to get drunk, didn't have to take the pills or the ride. Today, she could press charges; it could be considered rape. Was there something

I could have done? Should I have stopped her from taking a ride with those guys? The fact that she hadn't told me right away but had waited until I was making love to her, that made it even worse. I had a hard time looking at her the same way after that. Years later I still feel weird about it.

We both quit our jobs at the nightclub. We couldn't work there anymore. I had been thinking of finding a teaching job. I saw an ad and applied to an International School in Iran that was interviewing in Boston and I got a job offer on the spot. They would fly me over and set me up with a place. It was a two-year contract. I decided to take it. I didn't ask Kate if she wanted to come. I told her I thought we needed some time apart. I was no longer sure whether I wanted to marry her.

Once I got to Iran, I threw myself into the teaching job and learning about Iranian culture. I took classes in Persian and made friends with my Iranian landlord and his son. At the same time, I didn't want to cut off communication with Kate. We kept in touch by letter and a year later she asked if she could come join me. After a year in the Middle East, I was ready to give her another chance. I picked her up at the airport in Tehran. A week later she got hired as a secretary by Bell helicopter. It was easy for Americans to find work there then. It was an intense time to be there—1978.

There were demonstrations in the streets against the American-backed Shah. Americans began leaving in droves. Kate and I were living together but there was a distance between us now. One night Kate and I returned home from a party just before the 9 o'clock curfew and as we were walking up the stairs to our house in the northern section of the city, a military jeep pulled up and shined a spotlight on us and with a megaphone asked us where we were going.

From behind us a rifle shot rang out. I looked up and saw my landlord's son, Ali, on the roof, aiming his rifle at the soldiers in the jeep. The soldiers fired back at him and us. Kate and I dropped to the ground and crawled into our house.

The next day, Kate, who was still shaking, told me she planned to take a Bell Helicopter offer to fly her home to the U.S. I realized it was not going to work out between us. She had dumped her boyfriend Will to be with me. I had gone behind my friend's back to be with her. We'd both been with other people. She had gotten drunk and been raped or had sex with my co-workers. I had left her in the U.S. to teach in Iran. It was just too much drama. I dropped her at the airport. A month later I bribed a couple of Iranian soldiers at the airport and took a U.S. Airforce evacuation plane to Greece. I was in no rush to get back to the United States. Kate and I still kept in touch by letter. She found an apartment and a job as a secretary.

When I got back a month later, I took a cab to the apartment. A guy answered the door. He told me he'd let her know I dropped by.

GIRL NEXT DOOR

We met in a nightclub in 1979 and by nightclub, I mean a bar with pool tables and live music. She was preppy with a freshly ironed white blouse, jeans, light make-up and medium-length blond hair. She wore simple, understated jewelry. She seemed a little out of place at Great Scott's in Allston. I would not have spoken to her, but she was hanging around the pool table watching me win, and when she smiled, I could see she was really nice. Her smile made her look like the youngest kid in the family. It was a genuine unself-conscious smile, a Holly-go-lightly smile.

"Would you like to play partners?" I asked her.

Her name was Betsy. She offered me a Marlboro—you could smoke in clubs then. I was a social smoker. I bought her a glass of wine and after we lost at pool, (she was terrible) we danced to Heidi and the Secret Admirers. When she danced, she knew how to move her hips in a way that was sensuous without being slutty. I asked her where she lived.

"The North End," she said and I said, "Really? Me too." I asked if she could give me a ride home.

"Sure," she said.

I let my friend Richard know that I was leaving with her and wouldn't need a ride from him.

The North End of Boston is small enough that you can walk around it. "What street do you live on?" I asked when we got out of her Honda.

"Charter," she said.

"Really? I live on Charter too." I was starting to get nervous.

"What number?" I asked.

"Fifteen," she said.

I gulped. I lived one door up, at seventeen.

When she invited me in for a drink I was surprised. "It won't take you long to walk from here," she said and laughed.

The next day, I wanted to see her again, but her living so close kind of freaked me out. If we dated, and it didn't work out, it would be awkward. It almost felt like it was fate meeting someone who lived right next door—not that I believed in fate. I decided I should not see her for a few days. Then I bumped into her on the street a week later and we made a date to go to a movie.

We went to *Apocalypse Now,* and we met a friend of mine there. He happened to be a priest. I think that threw her a little. Afterward, we found a bar in the North End and talked about the movie. Maybe they should have called it "Post-Apocalypse Now," she said and laughed. She said she liked the movie but Brando was totally over the top. "I liked the references to *The Heart of Darkness* though: The Horror!"

I was impressed. She was smart, with her own opinions We started going out a couple of times a week.

A few months later we moved in together. I was bartending and looking for a teaching job. She was a secretary. There weren't many teaching jobs then or to put it more accurately, there were so many young people looking for teaching jobs, I couldn't find one. I applied for a job at the Sheraton Hotel. They had a training program for waiters for an upscale "nouvelle-cuisine" restaurant. Meanwhile, Betsy started taking courses at night for an MBA at BU. She was working for an art consultant during the day. The restaurant at the Sheraton, Apley's, was a big hit with the food critics. Julia Child even showed up for a meal.

Betsy and I moved out to Brighton, just outside of Boston to save on rent. A couple of years went by. She finished her degree.

I picked a bottle of pink champagne and some roses. I gave her a ring my mother had given to me and I asked her to marry me. She said yes and we set a tentative date. Then I started thinking, *Was she really the person for me? Maybe there was someone else out there better.* By then I was a Captain at the restaurant, making pretty good money. And there was a girl there, Connie, who was flirting with me. A cute 19-year-old. After work, a few of us from the restaurant would go across the street for drinks. One night, Connie showed up. She asked me to walk her home.

I started dropping by her apartment in the afternoon. At first it was great. It made me happy and I fooled myself into believing it was cool, but within a couple of weeks I realized that it was a mistake. I was acting like a jerk and it was completely unfair to Betsy, so I told Connie we had to stop the trysts. She had a meltdown when I left her apartment. She didn't show up for work for a week. Then she began calling me at the house in Brighton. Whenever Betsy picked up the phone, Connie hung up. "That's it!" Betsy said when she caught on. She threw the ring at me and moved out that weekend.

Betsy and I had both had had serious relationships before we met. She'd lived with a guy named Lenny that she'd gone out with in college. She said they did not survive the transition to the real world after they graduated. I'd had a wild, on-off affair with the girlfriend of one of my roomies in grad school. A couple of months after we broke up, I met Betsy. I think we were both a little cautious about long-term commitments.

When Betsy moved out of the apartment in Brighton, I wasn't entirely sure what I wanted. One of the women I worked with at the restaurant, Rosanne, said: "You have to look at it as a deal. Is she the best deal for you?" That seemed crass but if you changed "deal" to "person," it made sense. The more I thought about it, the more I realized that Betsy was a great catch—the best person for me. Meanwhile, Connie had started going out with my busboy, Milton. That was fine with me.

A couple of months later I called Betsy up, we met for coffee, and we decided to try again. I agreed to go to counseling. It was in the counseling sessions that it hit me how much we loved each other.

I quit my job at the restaurant. Between the hours and the temptation, restaurants are tough on relationships and I wanted to get into teaching. I found a job at a community college. Six months later we were married.

My wife has two personas. At work she goes by Elizabeth. There she is well-organized, efficient, a successful project manager and principal in an architectural firm. At home she is Betsy: an out-going, enthusiastic, upbeat person who loves soul and gospel.

I think what happens if you stay together and enjoy each other's company, respect each other, support each other, is that you grow loyal. I don't know how she feels about it, but I feel like I owe her big-time. For sticking with me. For supporting my writing, for thinking teaching is a worthwhile job, for cheering me on when I run in races even when I finish in the middle of the pack. I still find her attractive. Finding someone attractive is partly related, as you probably know, to how you feel about the person. When we got married, I remember saying, "We'll try it for five years and see where we are." Forty years later, we're still together.

MELODY 1954-2011

"What have you done with the garden entrusted to you?"
Antonio Machado

I've been thinking about that line from Vallejo lately. A friend of mine, Melody Edwardson, died in her sleep. In many cases, dying in one's sleep without warning might be preferable, but Melody was 57. She left behind two children, a son 23 and daughter 21. What made Melody's death difficult to deal with is that most of her life, particularly her adult life, was a struggle, and just when she seemed to be beginning to enjoy some success, her life ended.

Melody and my wife Elizabeth were friends in college. I met her when she was going to New England School of Law. My wife was going to BU for an MBA. I was bartending and substitute teaching. We were all living in the North End of Boston at the time—the early eighties. The three of us would have pizza at Regina's and catch a Celtics game. It was easy to get tickets in those days. Melody was a big Celtics fan.

After law school Melody moved back home to Saratoga Springs. She worked as a legal guardian for children. She hadn't been home for long when her mother died (her father had left her mother years before). Melody met Frank, who worked at the harness track, they fell in love and married. Soon they had two kids. Then, Frank divorced her and married his administrative assistant. In an ugly divorce settlement, he accused Melody of being an unfit mother. He had taken videos of the house when it was a mess. Melody was a terrible housekeeper. And Melody had just been diagnosed with Graves's disease causing her eyes to bug out. She didn't look like herself. The judge awarded the children to Frank. He kept them for a year then realized he didn't want them and sent them back to live with Melody. She was the one who raised them. She continued to work as a legal guardian until the Great Recession.

When the recession of 2007 wound down, Melody decided to try her luck at headhunting—recruiting people for jobs on commission. She was good at it, but it's a slow business built through networking. Meanwhile, her son Colin had won a hockey scholarship to Lake Forest College, but he burnt out on hockey, quit the team and left school. He moved back home with Melody and went to work in a factory. Colin was able to help out with the rent. Meanwhile, Melody helped her daughter get into an art education program at Alfred College and managed to pull together enough money in loans and financial aid to enable her daughter to go. At this point Melody was living commission to commission. When her car broke down, she couldn't afford to get it fixed. She pedaled around on her bicycle. Then, finally, she began to turn the corner: her business slowly gained momentum. Her son was working full time and her daughter was graduating from college. Her garden wasn't exactly flourishing but there were sprouts.

Despite the fact that she had struggled so much of her life, she prevailed. She never gave up. She always remained sanguine, upbeat even: "good at being in the moment and really savoring a book, a movie, a meal or a terrific martini," she said in an email. My wife had written her to vent about being a woman over fifty surrounded by young people at work and feeling invisible and Melody had responded with the aforementioned and the following: "you enjoy the smaller stuff like the smell of an herb garden or the feel of the sun on the back of your head as you sit in your

Adirondack chair. You have some perspective; you are horrified by wrinkles and it all going south, so you hardly notice that you hate your nose or your eyebrows. Without glasses you can't see your nose or your eyebrows anyway, so who cares?" She had this sardonic, self-deprecating way of supporting her friends.

"Being invisible isn't all bad," she said. "They don't see you stealing canapes at the cocktail party." Melody liked her martinis and she loved to entertain. Every year, my wife and I would visit her in Saratoga in August and we'd go to the track together, admire the horses and scour the papers for long shots. Melody had remained a Celtics fan and she and I would talk about players and trades as we watched the beautiful thoroughbreds run.

Melody wasn't quite pretty but when she was younger, she was attractive with a heart-shaped face and a devilish smile and she knew how to dress. As a child, before her parents had divorced, she'd lived in one of the mansions that line Broadway on the road out to Skidmore College. One of her friends described her as very Episcopalian--an Episcopalian who loved a dry martini with olives.

According to the American Dream, if we follow our passion and work hard, we marry, have children and achieve success. If we cultivate our garden, by the time we reach fifty, we harvest the rewards. Melody followed her passion, worked hard, married and had children, but her husband left her; she struggled for years to achieve success and when she was close, she died.

My wife and I learned of her death from Eve, another college friend. Melody's sister had survived a pulmonary embolism and the thinking was that was the cause of Melody's untimely demise. A pulmonary embolism is caused by "blood clots that travel to the lungs." If she was still married, her husband could have driven her to a hospital where doctors could have dissolved the blood clot. Her son and daughter were asleep in other rooms in the house. It was her daughter that found her. Fitzgerald says, "we beat on, boats against the current," but sometimes the current is just too strong.

UNTIL THE END

My two sisters, Susan and Dottie, work with the hospice nurse to give my father a sponge bath. Susan is a nurse. She's taken leave from work to care for my father just as my wife's sister had taken care of her mother, and my friend's sister took care of her mother.

My father is skeletal. Ribs protrude like the rungs of a ladder. His legs wooden and shiny as if shellacked. When he breathes, there's a rattle.

Two weeks prior, Susan had an ambulance deliver my father to her apartment from a nursing rehab. The doctors said it was a matter of days before he would pass away. My father had stopped eating. His doctors wanted to put in a feeding tube, but my dad was still mentally sharp and he was adamant about not having one—no feeding tube, and "do not resuscitate." My father, my sisters and I had all learned from our experience with my mother.

My mother had gone into the hospital for an operation on her kidneys, but complications ensued. She had her gall bladder removed; then she needed an operation on her heart. One day we walked into the hospital to find her hooked up to a feeding tube despite the fact that we had told her doctor she did not want one. "It could help her recover," he said to us. Then my sisters convinced my dad to allow it. It is one thing to request no feeding tube before one is inserted. Requiring doctors to remove it, puts the onus on the family.

My mother did not recover. Instead, over a period of months she slowly died while being shuffled between the hospital and a nursing home. The experts counseling us were of course profiting from her treatment. At first, they were paid by Medicaid, and then by my father. The last nursing home my mother stayed in was filled four to a room with dependent elderly. Most were on feeding tubes, suffering from dementia or Alzheimer's. No one wants to end up in that situation.

My father outlived my mother by two years. I helped him move out of the spacious two bed-room apartment he had lived in with my mother into a 300 square foot one bedroom in an assisted living apartment complex. My sister Dottie would visit him there and take him for walks during the week. My wife and I would treat him to a breakfast or a dinner out on Saturdays. He liked to try new food so we'd go to a Thai or Vietnamese or Indian restaurant. He seemed to enjoy that. My other sister, Susan, would visit him on Sundays and take him to mass.

My father was a quiet, loyal guy who did not make new friends easily and the few friends he did have had died. We were told that he usually ate by himself in the common dining room. One of my aunts also lived in the same assisted living apartment complex, but she was a little too cheery for him. Soon after he moved in, he sold his car after getting pulled over by police a number of times for missing stop signs and going through red lights. He had also owned motor boats for most of his adult life, but those were all long gone. He didn't have a lot on his plate.

It became clear to my sisters and me that he was depressed. My mother was the upbeat one who loved family parties, drives to the shore, dinners out. He had devoted himself to taking care of her, especially at the end of her life when he spent a lot of time bringing her to doctors, picking up her medicine, keeping her company. A happily-married couple can become overly dependent on each other and that was the case with my parents. Once she died, he seemed a little lost. Taking care of my mother had given his life purpose and now he was like a rudderless boat.

My sisters and I convinced him to take anti-depressants and to follow a routine of getting out for a walk every day. With the support he was getting from us, and the medication, his mood began to improve.

Just after his 87th birthday, he seemed to be emerging from depression when he began to fall. First, he bruised his arm. Next, he broke a couple of ribs. The third time, he cracked vertebrae. In the hospital, he contracted pneumonia. He was transferred to a rehab and that's when he stopped eating and my sister Susan had him delivered to her apartment.

She set him up in the living room. For about a week, with help from my sister Dottie, she fed him and cared for him and he seemed to be recovering. He started eating again, sitting up and talking, and, with my sisters' help, he was able to get up out of bed and sit in a chair. He was visited by his grandchildren and his great grandchildren. Then, he appeared to decide he was ready to go; he stopped eating altogether and began to fade away.

So, I was there, that Sunday, two weeks after he arrived at my sister's apartment, as a visitor. He was on morphine and seemed to be asleep although Susan said he could hear us. Hearing, she said, is the last sense to go. When it was time to change him, she asked me to step out of the room. This was apparently to protect me from seeing my dad naked. When I returned, I held his hand a said a few words to him. That night, a few hours after I had left, my father died.

So, this is partly a cautionary tale about experiences with doctors, hospitals, and nursing homes, but it is also a tribute to my sisters for doing what each of us would like done and how and where we would like to be when we're ready to go. And it's a tribute to all those daughters and nurses who care for our mothers and fathers, who feed them and change them and hold their hands until the end.

A HEADMASTER'S STORY

At Augustin Preparatory School, the independent Catholic high school where I taught, the headmaster was not only the director of education, he also thought of himself as our spiritual leader. In addition, he needed to be a fundraiser. Most importantly, he represented the face of the school. Not an easy role to fulfill. Austin Prep was founded by Augustinian Friars as a boys' school in 1961 and began accepting girls ten years later. When I started teaching there in 2000, there were 600 students in grades 1-12. Austin is a moderately priced school in Reading, Massachusetts with students from the surrounding suburbs.

Our headmaster, Peter, came into the job as a temporary replacement just before I got there, when the previous headmaster died. Peter was a very religious, compassionate guy who came from Dorchester, an Irish working-class section of Boston. He never quite left Dorchester behind and that alone would almost do him in. I liked him because he allowed us teachers the freedom to design our own curriculum as long as we included a moral dimension to our classes. Peter's biggest flaw from our point of view was that he was a slow processor and he wouldn't make changes fast enough. He was skeptical about technology and reluctant to adopt it. In retrospect, he may have been onto something. The Board was always worried about fundraising and enrollment which they thought was based on our image. They thought Peter's resistance to investing in new technology hurt fundraising and enrollment. But that isn't what brought him down. Catholic Schools are very sensitive about what the public thinks. Part of our mission included educating morally enlightened students.

The first year I was at Augustin I was sitting in the cafeteria at a faculty meeting in October. Peter made a few announcements about coming meetings; he was about to dismiss us when one of the guidance counselors, Kevin Riley, asked if he could address the meeting. Reluctantly, Peter handed him the mike. Kevin was a wiry guy in his mid-seventies.

Why hadn't he retired? I wondered.

Kevin launched into a rant about a faculty fund that was apparently handled by the administration. Kevin said funds were missing or misused. I couldn't really follow it, but as he was talking, Peter stood up, said "That's enough!" and he strode up to Kevin and attempted to wrest the mike away from him.

Kevin pulled the mike back. He was a strong old guy. But Peter, who was around sixty, probably outweighed Kevin by fifty pounds, and he was a few inches taller. He grabbed Kevin's arm and they struggled. Peter turned deep red as he tried to take the mike from Kevin. It was beginning to look like the Wide World of Wrestling. Would Peter pick Kevin up over his head and toss him into the audience? Or would Kevin surprise Peter with a karate chop that would send him reeling?

Suddenly Kevin kind of froze, turned grey/blue and collapsed onto the floor.

Peter stood hulking over him. I could see that Kevin was breathing, but he appeared to be unconscious.

"Call an ambulance!" one of my colleagues shouted.

It took about ten minutes for the EMTs to arrive. In the meantime, Kevin slowly came to though he seemed groggy. We found out the next day that he had had a stroke.

Three months later there was a trial. Kevin was suing Peter and the school. It seemed to me that it was clearly Peter's fault. We happened to have the day of the trial off and I went and sat in back. Peter's lawyer called two witnesses. One was a colleague of mine from the English department. David had almost become a priest but found he couldn't go through with it and Peter had hired him to give him a shot at teaching. He was an overweight, nervous redhead who always seemed to be sweating. The other witness was Peter's Assistant, a single, unmarried middle-aged, overweight woman who looked a little like Linda Ronstadt. She appeared to be in love with our headmaster based on the way she gazed at him. Both witnesses testified that Peter had absolutely nothing to do with Kevin's stroke. According to them, Peter walked up to Kevin after he had already had a stroke to help. They claimed that he never grabbed Kevin or pulled the microphone away from him. According to them, Kevin simply collapsed on his own. In other words, they lied.

Kevin, who appeared to have recovered, made the classic mistake of hiring a fool for a lawyer, that is, himself, and he had no witnesses. He should have gotten a lawyer and arrived in court in a wheelchair. He apparently thought people would actually tell the truth, but as you probably know by now, in trials as in other walks in life, people seldom tell the truth. The judge ruled against Kevin. There was no jury. It was what is called a bench trial.

Nonetheless, the board came to a settlement with Kevin, covering his hospital expenses and giving him 75K as part of a retirement package. He was told he had to leave the school immediately. So, although the Board didn't like paying off Kevin Riley, the story was kept quiet. It never made it to the papers or to the students and their parents. Nonetheless, it was a strike against Peter.

Over the next ten years of my tenure, there were a couple of potential scandals that Peter managed to cover up. A popular senior boy was caught with an 8th grader. He was 18 and she was 13. He'd driven her home after a co-ed track practice that included the middle school team. He followed her into her house claiming he just wanted to use the bathroom. No one was home.

That night she told her older sister she'd been abused and her sister convinced her to tell her parents. Rather than going to the police, the parents of the girl went to Peter and asked what they should do. Peter assured them that he would handle it. Peter was very good at expressing empathy and connecting with parents. He also had an authoritative air. He suspended the boy and didn't allow him to go to the Prom.

One spring day a student called in a bomb scare to Peter's office and posted a hit list of students and teachers on social media. Peter ignored both threats. He met with the student's parents and told them he'd keep an eye on their son. The boy took the post down.

One event that ticked off the Board occurred when one of the Board members, using the faculty bathroom, walked in on a sophomore boy having sex with a freshman girl. That boy was suspended for an entire week! There were meetings between Peter and the Board. The Board was appalled. Not just that a 16-year-old boy was having sex with a 15-year-old girl, but that they were doing it in the faculty bathroom! And this had happened under Peter's watch! What if the story got out?

But the story did not get out. What cooked our headmaster's goose was a rap song written by a student in my English class. It was a catchy number and my student Tim sent it to a local radio station that played it. Soon it was getting requested. The problem was that the song used the word "rape." It wasn't clear if it referred to an actual rape or not. A reporter from the *Boston Globe* picked up on it and one morning when I arrived at school, there were reporters with cameras in the parking lot. Peter called Tim down to his office that day. He was told not to talk to reporters (as were the faculty) and he was suspended for a week. When he came back, he apologized to the entire school at an assembly.

This was, apparently, the final straw for the Board. Peter had embarrassed the school. Moral dimension! Fundraising! The fact that Peter had also been dragging his feet about adopting new technology didn't help either.

So, Peter was fired. I had mixed feelings about it. He had hired me and allowed me to teach what I wanted to teach and was generally supportive. Even when Tim wrote the song that got him fired, he didn't blame me. But he, in the tradition of the Catholic Church, covered up any crimes involving sex and he got away with causing someone to have a stroke. I wasn't really sorry to see him go, but that that before they hired his replacement.

THE BOAT PEOPLE

It was an assembly with all 600 students of the Catholic school at which I taught sitting on folding chairs in the gym. We had been told that the speaker had escaped from Cambodia to Thailand in the late 1970s. Our students were well-behaved at these gatherings. They were always happy to get out of class. They sat quietly, the boys in white polos and slacks, the girls in plaid skirts and white shirts. The teachers sat with them or stood at the ends of the rows to keep an eye on them. The speaker, who had a high-pitched voice, was a thin fifty-something male with short, dark hair, an ill-fitting sports jacket and a red tie. His tone was upbeat.

"My family and I lived in a village in the countryside of Cambodia," he told us. "My father and mother were out in the rice paddy working. My brother and I were at home playing together. I was five years old and he was two years older." He smiled and nodded.

Our students, although they were quiet, were not really engaged or interested. They whispered to each other. We gave them stern looks and shushed them. They ignored us.

"I remember hearing trucks come into the village," the speaker continued. "My brother and I jumped up and ran outside to see what was going on."

I was thinking of another story of a Vietnamese student from a college class I'd taught a couple of years before. He had also been a refugee. One of a number of Vietnamese who had escaped by boat and who had made his way to Australia and then to the United States where he grew up with a family in Massachusetts who adopted him. But I wanted to listen to the story of the man onstage.

"The trucks were open in the back and filled with kids who were singing and cheering. 'Come, join us,' they called. "In the front seat of the truck sat two soldiers in uniforms. 'Climb up,' the kids said to my brother and me. Other children from our village climbed up the sides of the truck. 'Let's go,' my brother said to me. It will be an adventure.'"

'We'll bring you back by dinner,' a soldier said getting out of the truck. He lifted my brother and then me up into the back with the others. As we drove off, we sang together."

The Vietnamese student I had in class had told his story in a personal essay. In 1975, just after the Americans left, his mother had packed food and clothes in sacks, and left their village with her two children in the middle of the night. My student was a little older than the Cambodian speaker had been—he was seven in 1975. His younger sister was just two, so his mother had to carry her. His father had been killed in the war. This was in South Vietnam. His mother wanted to get them out before the North Vietnamese took over the country. I turned my attention back to the speaker.

"The soldiers brought us to a camp," he said. "We spent the next five years there. They trained us to be soldiers like them to fight the enemy. I was too young to fight when we got there but my brother was taught how to shoot a rifle right away. Later we fought together for the Party." He smiled and nodded.

I suddenly realized he meant the Communist Party and that he must have been fighting for Pol Pot. The dictator, with the help of the Khmer Rouge, was responsible for the deaths of almost two million Cambodians. So, the speaker was one of his soldiers.

The speaker told us his brother was an excellent soldier who died in a battle when he was 12 years old.

I thought again of my Vietnamese student. My student, Han, wrote that it took ten days to reach the coast. They slept during the day and traveled at night. His mother used the stars to guide them. She gave all the food she had brought to her children. She grew weaker by the day, but she pushed on. When they reached the coast, the mother collapsed and dying, handed Han's sister to him. He found a boat that was leaving and got his sister onboard, but within hours, she died in his arms. She was taken from him and set adrift. He watched her sink.

The boat made it to Indonesia where Han stayed until he was sponsored by an American family living outside of Boston. Fifteen years later he sat in my Composition class at Stonehill College.

"Five years later," the man onstage said, "I escaped with friends to Thailand where we lived in a camp for two years. From there, I was adopted by an American family in Wisconsin. It was difficult at first, learning English but eventually we succeeded! And now, here I am giving talks about my experience. I am very happy to be here, in America."

He stepped back from the podium and the headmaster walked across the stage to shake his hand.

We understood that we were supposed to clap and we did. The students always used these opportunities to clap loudly and yell support because they were so restrained in class.

The headmaster dismissed us by rows and we filed back to the main building. The students walked slowly to reduce the amount of time they would spend in class. When all my students returned, I asked them what they thought of the assembly.

"It was hard to understand him," Joe said and everyone nodded except for the one Asian student in the class, Chloe Kim. I talked for a few minutes about the war in Vietnam and about what happened in Cambodia. I told them that almost two million Cambodians had been killed by the Khmer Rouge—the government then in control. "The Khmer Rouge was recently brought to trial but only three people were convicted of war crimes." It was last period. Their minds were elsewhere.

I was trying to reconcile the two different stories of refugees in my mind. I had always felt sympathetic to refugees from Southeast Asia, partly because of the story of my Vietnamese student. It might be the saddest story I had ever heard. I remember him crying when he read his essay about it in class. Hell, half the class was crying, me included. But this new story about the Cambodian who had been kidnapped to fight for Pol Pot was, in some ways, even worse. How many Cambodians had he and his brother killed? And could I really blame them? They were just children.

The bell rang. Soon my room was empty.

ANDRÉA

Her name was Andrea but she pronounced it as if it were Spanish: Ahn-dray-uh. She was tall with long red hair and freckles, a healthy American girl. I'd had her two older sisters and they were both excellent students. I'd written glowing recommendations for them that helped assure their admittance to Georgetown where their mother had gone. I was favorably disposed to the Randall family.

Near the end of the first quarter of Honors Composition Andréa asked for a recommendation for early admission to Georgetown and I wrote it, though I didn't have much to go on. It was a week after that when the class assignment was to talk for a few minutes about an artist and a work of art the students liked. It was an easy assignment to get students comfortable presenting to a group. I brought a copy of The Milkmaid by Vermeer up on the Smart Board and talked about the use of color and light and how it made an ordinary scene and a milkmaid, beautiful. I talked briefly about Vermeer and when it was painted.

The next class met the following week and it happened that Andréa was the last one to go. She asked if she could do it the following class. Ok, I said. They were seniors and really busy after all.

At the beginning of the next class I asked if she was ready and she said, "I already did it, last week."

The class went silent.

"Ah no, you did not," I said. I was kind of at a loss for a few seconds then I said, "see me after class."

After class Andréa insisted that she had already presented.

"Andréa," I said," that's crazy. I'll have to give you an F for the assignment."

She stood, smiled, and walked out.

The next afternoon her mother appeared in my room just after the bell for the end of last period rang. Her mother was tall, thin, and stern with pale skin and red hair pulled tightly back. She wore a pencil skirt, a white blouse, and heels.

I stood up. "Mrs. Randall." I gestured to a chair beside my desk.

She took a seat. Her jaw was clenched.

"Did you call my daughter schizophrenic?" She asked.

"No," I said. I told her about Andréa claiming she'd done a class presentation when she hadn't and then sticking to the story after class. I did say "that's crazy" to her.

"Obviously you're mistaken," Mrs. Randall said.

"Mrs. Randall, I just wrote Andréa a recommendation and you know I thought both of her sisters were excellent students. Why would I make this up?"

"How should I know," she said. "She's calling herself Andréa?" She drummed her fingers on my desk. "I see I'll have to talk to Peter about it. I just got back from Georgetown where I had to meet with Rebecca's Composition teacher. He gave her a warning at the midterm. Then I met with the dean who assured me he would talk with her professor."

It took a few seconds for that to sink in. She'd visited Georgetown to straighten out her daughter's professor.

Peter was my Headmaster. I met with him that Friday.

He said I could go ahead and flunk Andréa for the assignment but that beyond that, I should just let it go. Peter was a reasonable guy. He stood and we shook hands.

After winter break the seniors were talking in my class during activity period about Christmas. "My sisters were both home from Georgetown," Andréa said." The first night at dinner, Rebecca and Kate texted me under the table about sneaking out later that night. My mother saw us, said "No Way! Give me those phones!" She took our phones and locked them in the safe in my father's study.

"But we knew the combo so later that night we got the phones back when my mother went to bed. In the morning though, she came into our rooms, found us on our phones in bed, and she took them away again. She said we'd get them back when we left for school."

Andréa looked over at me. She didn't seem to mind that I was listening.

"Then she tells us as punishment there would be no gifts for us for Christmas. She said she'd drop some of them off at the Salvation Army. She had also bought us Celtics tickets and she told us she was giving them away to her friends." Andréa laughed. "She's out of her mind." She smiled. She had a great smile. She looked at me and I just shook my head.

A few weeks later, Andréa thanked me when she got into Georgetown on early admission. She told me her mother had bought a condo near campus so she could keep an eye on her and her sisters. "I'm thinking of taking a gap year," Andréa said. "Do you think I should?"

I started nodding then stopped myself. I thought gap years were good for students. But in this case, I was not about to say anything.

THE WRONG WAY HOME

It was a beautiful night in June in Boston. My wife and I were celebrating my 60th birthday with dinner at a French restaurant called *Des Jardins*. It was warm enough to sit on the patio outside. I had a Sidecar and she ordered a glass of champagne. We toasted to a good year. I'd had a book of poems published and she'd finished the project she managed with the new Boston School Department Headquarters in Roxbury. "To progress!" she said raising her glass.

After dinner we decided to stroll along the Charles River. There was a Pointer Sisters free concert at the Hatch Shell. We could stop there, listen to a few songs and then ramble along the river to the T stop at Charles Street and take the train back to our condo in Somerville.

There was only one Pointer sister left but she had her daughter and her niece to accompany her so "Let's Get Excited" had the crowd dancing. The moon rose above its twin in the Charles, sailboats glided by and the crowd at the concert seemed lively and buoyant. There were a couple of hundred people there—a mixed group of young and old, and a few families.

We started making our way along the river path toward the Charles Street train station at around 9:30. It is a little less than a mile from the hatch shell to the T. It was a clear night and the moonlight illuminated our path, but there wasn't much in the way of lighting other than that. In fact, it was pretty dark just off the walkway. I had begun to wonder if walking along the Charles at night was such a good idea when out of the corner of my eye, I saw two figures rustling a row of bushes.

A young white guy with black hair wearing white shorts and no shirt or shoes suddenly stepped out of the darkness and said to me: "Don't look at me." He appeared agitated as if he had been caught doing something wrong.

It was impossible not to look at him.

"Did you say something to me?" he said.

"No" I said. "I didn't say anything." I glanced at my wife, took her arm and picked up the pace.

"I told you not to look at me," he said walking behind us.

He was in his twenties, thin, with dark eyes. He seemed angry and wound up. He could have been drunk or juiced on drugs. I walked faster to put a little distance between us, but I kept glancing back at him to see what he was up to.

He undid his belt, pulled it off and wrapped it around his hand.

At that point, had I been on my own, I would have run. I'm a runner and can run pretty fast if I have to, but with my wife there, dressed up, with heels on, that was not an option.

I turned to face him in order to keep myself between my wife and him and I kept moving. I was walking backward now. We were about a half a mile from the concert. I didn't see anyone else around. "Leave us alone," I said to him.

He began running at me with the belt raised. I set my feet and swung at him, connecting with his jaw just as he reached me. He went down. I thought maybe I had knocked him out. My wife was crying. I held her arm and walked quickly with her along the path toward the train. When I looked back over my shoulder though, I saw the young guy being helped up by someone else, another bigger guy. This must have been who he was in the bushes with. Were they shooting up? Or having sex? I was worried that they would both come after us.

But the big guy turned back and disappeared into the darkness once he'd helped my attacker to his feet. "I'm going to kill you," the young guy yelled at me and began running toward us again.

I had a pocket knife with me. I took it out and pried the blade out. "I have a knife," I called. "Stay the hell away from us!"

He charged right at me.

I swiped at him defensively with the knife and cut him superficially just above his belly button.

"You stabbed me!" He said incredulously.

Meanwhile, my wife had taken out her phone and was calling the police. That was something we should have done right away. Maybe that's what my attacker's friend had gone to do.

The young guy came toward me again.

I backed up, holding the knife in front of me, telling him to keep away. Now he seemed to be losing energy. He stumbled a little and swayed.

A few minutes later, the State Police drove their car onto the path behind me. They have a station right at the end of the Charles River, near the Museum of Science.

As two policemen got out of their car, my assailant called out: "He stabbed me," then he swooned and collapsed onto the pavement.

"Did you stab him?" one of the cops asked me.

"Yes," I said. "He attacked me." I still had the knife in my hand. The cop grabbed my wrist, taking the knife. Then he pulled me around and clamped handcuffs on me behind my back. He pushed my head down and shoved me into the back seat of the cruiser.

My wife was crying hysterically outside the car.

An ambulance had pulled up and I watched the medics pick the young guy up, put him on a stretcher and load him into the back. They had a short trip to Mass General Hospital just across Storrow Drive. One of the troopers drove me to the state police station while the other stayed behind at the scene. He had told the cop who put me in the car that he would look for witnesses.

At the station, another trooper took my fingerprints. A detective asked me if I wanted to make a statement. The situation, although obvious from my point of view, wasn't so clear from the perspective of someone showing up when my attacker went into a swoon. It looked like I was the assailant. I decided I should keep quiet until I had a lawyer.

A trooper locked me in a cell. He told me I was lucky; it had been a slow night and I could have a cell to myself.

They took my wife into another room to get a statement from her.

If the police had arrived a few minutes earlier, my attacker might have been the one arrested, but when they showed up, it looked bad for me. In fact, it looked as if I had been the aggressor. Now I was in an 8 X 6 cell with a metal door and bullet proof glass. The bed was a metal slab. There was a toilet and an overhead camera.

I blamed myself. I never should have walked along the Charles River at night with my wife. In retrospect, I realized that I was putting her in danger. That's why I had a knife with me, but now I wished I hadn't brought a knife. I probably could have fought him off. I'm glad I didn't have a gun. If I had had a gun, I might have shot him. That would have been much worse. As it was, I was charged with a felony: assault with a dangerous weapon.

My wife returned a couple of hours later with bail. It was $1000; she had had to go to a few ATMs to get it. The sergeant released me and told me the arraignment would be Monday at the Charlestown Courthouse. When I got back home, I called a few friends for lawyer recommendations. The first lawyer I talked to told me he thought he could make a deal with the D.A. If I were to plead guilty, he claimed he could get me off with probation, no jail time. But I would have a felony on my record. If you are charged with a felony, you can no longer vote and it is hard to find a job. Every time you apply, you have to write your arrest record on the application. It would mean the end of my job teaching at the Catholic school or teaching anywhere else for that matter. One of the friends I called, a former cop, told me he knew a good lawyer he'd seen in action over the years. He gave me his name; I looked him up and called him. I told him what happened and he agreed to meet in court that Monday in Charlestown.

I called in sick that morning. The Charlestown Courthouse is an imposing brick building over a hundred years old situated right in the square. My wife and I met my lawyer, Steve Sacks, just inside the courthouse. Sacks is a short, thin, grey-haired guy. He wore a grey suit. He had glasses and stooped a bit. He told us he had read the police report and he had learned that the Assistant DA had considered indicting me for attempted murder but her boss had talked her out of it. Steve had a report from the hospital. The victim's name was Tommy S--------. He was twenty-six years old. He had told the nurse at the hospital that he had been drinking all day. He received twelve stitches for his wound. He had left the hospital that night and walked back across Storrow Drive to the police station and filled out a report alleging that he had seen my wife and me arguing and he intervened thinking I might be about to harm her. According to him, that was when I attacked him.

I told my lawyer my story. He seemed pretty skeptical. He said not too much would happen that day. I would plead not guilty. He would ask to have time to gather evidence and the judge would grant him that time.

On Monday the courthouse was almost empty. The judge was in his eighties and seemed kind of out of it. Judges can keep working for as long as they want to. Not really a great idea. The Assistant DA was a sexy blond in her thirties dressed in a short skirt. The judge loved staring at her.

The first case was a guy in chains who had robbed a 7-11. He was Black, around thirty years old. He stood up when charged with armed robbery and said, "I plead guilty, your Honor."

The judge laughed. "No, no, son," he said. "Do you have a lawyer?"

"No," the guy said.

"Ok, well, the court will appoint a lawyer for you. Meanwhile, you need to plead not guilty. Otherwise, I'm going to sentence you to ten years in prison, right now." The judge laughed.

'Ok, your honor, I'll plead not guilty."

"Miss James," the judge said to the DA. "Can you find a lawyer for this young man?"

"Yes, your honor," Miss James said. She smiled and the judge smiled back.

The judge called me forward and read the charges. I pleaded not guilty. My lawyer asked that I be released on my own recognizance. The DA objected but the judge ruled in my favor. The trial was set for three months later.

I was back at school the next day. Luckily for me, there was no mention of my arrest in the newspapers. I'm not sure why. Usually someone on *The Boston Globe* and *The Herald* covers local arrests and it would have made a catchy story: Catholic high school teacher arrested for a stabbing on the Charles River after leaving a Pointer Sisters' concert.

As a result, no-one knew about it at school. Yet two weeks later the headmaster showed up in my room at the end of the school day and told me he had received a letter from the diocese. He handed it to me. It cited my arrest and said I should be not be allowed in the classroom. The headmaster, though, was a supportive, compassionate guy and he asked me what happened. I told him my story.

"Ok," he said. "Keep me posted. In the meantime, you can continue to teach."

There were only a few days of school left before summer vacation started.

I met with my lawyer in late June. He told me that Tommy S-----. was on probation for possession of heroin. He was also involved in another trial about a robbery in a bar. He was a bartender. He had spent time in a juvenile detention center as a teen but his record was sealed. The hospital reported that he was inebriated when he checked in for stitches.

I returned to the Charlestown Courthouse in September.

Tommy did not show up. There was a new DA. This woman did not wear short skirts and did not flirt with the judge. My lawyer made a statement: "My client was walking along the Charles River with his wife when the plaintiff came out of the bushes and attacked him. He was defending himself and his wife and he did not seriously wound the plaintiff. It is a simple case of self-defense and it should be dismissed.

The judge asked the DA if she had anything to add. She said that sounded about right to her. She must have researched Tommy's record.

The judge dismissed the charges but said they would remain open for a year in case the plaintiff decided to appear in court or if new information came out.

I told my headmaster about the outcome and he seemed satisfied. So, it was all good, right?

I remembered that when I was trying to get away there was a voice behind him calling out "Leave the old guy alone!" That meant there was at least one witness. But whoever it was didn't come forward. If something like this had happened in the town where I grew up, Milton, the police would have known Tommy and me. They would not have believed his story. The way a situation appears when the police show up may not be reflective of what has occurred before they arrived.

We had taken the wrong way home, walked beyond the music and the crowds onto an unlit path at the edge of the river on a Saturday night. We had witnessed something we weren't supposed to see. So, we were attacked and when we tried to get away, we were pursued. When I knocked my assailant down, he got back up. When I told him I had a knife, and showed it to him, he charged at me. Did he want to be hurt or was he too high and drunk to care?

Well, he was clever enough that night to lie and manipulate the legal system and since the police didn't know us, they believed him. So did the first DA apparently.

My wife was able to post bail and we were able to afford a lawyer. The fee for my lawyer was two thousand. Not a lot of money, but more than the African-American guy charged with robbing a 7-11 was able to come up with. Also, my lawyer knew what he was doing. The first lawyer I spoke with advised me to admit to a felony in order to avoid jail. How many people charged with serious crimes accept deals to reduce the amount of time they will spend in jail and then end up with felonies on their record?

If a case is dismissed, why does it remain on your record? Even without a conviction, I now had a record of an arrest for assault with a dangerous weapon.

A couple of years later, I left the Catholic school when they hired a headmaster who pressured everyone over sixty to retire. He would have let me go when he found out about my arrest anyway, so I gave my notice. I thought I would have an easy time picking up part-time college teaching jobs since I have a couple of graduate degrees in English, experience teaching in college as well as high school, and long list of publications, but no takers. All the applications ask for a CORI (a criminal offender record of information). Would you want to hire or even work with someone who was arrested for assault with a dangerous weapon?

GRUDGES

My parents had the Coughlin's, Dan and my mother's sister, Eleanor, over to play cards once a month. I was allowed to come into the kitchen and watch as long as I didn't say anything. I liked to see who had the biggest pile of change. I was eleven. I understood the rules of poker. My uncle Dan usually won. He was a very confidant guy who always had a slight smile on his face. We liked each other. But he wasn't smiling that night. Even though he was winning, he seemed angry about something. My mother said he had a big job with the Boston Public Schools. Maybe it was a problem with work.

He was bald with angular features and a pointed chin. I thought he looked like an eagle. Much different from my father who was handsome with a full head of black hair and ocean blue, sensitive eyes. My mother, Eleanor's younger sister, was pretty with blond hair and a big laugh. Eleanor, who was not as attractive with dark hair and a round face, was out of sorts that night. She kept folding early, throwing in her cards.

"What the matter, El?" my mother asked.

"Oh, I lost my engagement ring," she said. "I've looked all over for it but it's gone. I feel awful about it."

"I told you to forget about it," Dan said. "I'll get you a new one."

"But it's my fault," aunt Eleanor said. She started to cry.

My mother went quiet. She seemed to be thinking about something. Hatching a plan probably.

The next day when I got home from school. My mother was in a good mood.

"You seem happy," I said.

"I had a great idea last night. You know how auntie El lost her ring. Well, your grandmother gave me her engagement ring before she died. I was holding onto it for when you got engaged but I thought, why not give it to aunt El? She was so upset about losing her ring. I went over to her house today and gave it to her.

Eleanor lived two blocks over from us. My mother and aunt El visited each other all the time and days they didn't visit, they talked on the phone.

My mother was already setting the table or dinner. "Wait," my mother said, "are you mad at me? Did you want me to save the ring for you?"

"Huh? Me, no, I don't care." I couldn't imagine what might happen in ten years. Then again, I didn't like the idea of my mother giving a ring away that I was supposed to get.

That night after my father got home and we were sitting down to a roast chicken dinner, there was a knock at the back door. My mother had already told my father about the ring and he said it was a good idea. I got up from the table and opened the door. It was uncle Dan.

He walked in and threw a ring on the table.

"Who the hell do you think you are?" he said to my mother. "Giving my wife an engagement ring. Like I said last night, I'll replace the ring. We don't need your charity." He held his bald head back and looked down his beak at my mom.

"But Dan," my father said, "Peg was just trying to help."

"You stay out of it," Dan said.

My father stood up and walked around the table.

"I think you'd better leave, Dan," he said.

Dan took a step toward him and I thought for a minute they were going to fight. But then Dan turned and left.

A few weeks later on card night, my parents sat alone at the kitchen table. My aunt and uncle didn't show up at 7 the way they always had.

"Well, that's ridiculous," my mother said.

"Dan is a real piece of work," my father was shuffling the cards.

"I guess they aren't going to come," my mother said. "Maybe I made a mistake."

They never played cards again. My uncle Dan did not speak to my parents for the next ten years. My mother sent a letter of apology to Dan; she and aunt El still spoke on the phone, but they stopped visiting each other.

Strangely enough, uncle Dan kept in touch with me. I was an athlete and he would come to my football games, basketball games and track meets. He'd wait for me and pat me on the shoulder and shake my hand but if my dad was there, he wouldn't say anything to him. It was pretty awkward.

He finally had a conversation with my father at the wake of my mother's brother. They shook hands. My mother cried and hugged my aunt, but they never were really close again. I found out later that my aunt had found her engagement ring a few days after the rift with my parents, but Dan remained mad anyway. She dropped the ring my mother had given her in our mailbox when we were out.

My uncle Dan wasn't the only one to hold a grudge in the family. When my younger brother moved from Boston to northern Maine, my parents never forgave him. So, my brother cut off ties with my parents and with me and my sisters because we remained close to my mother and father. When my parents died, he didn't even come down for the funeral. I haven't heard from him in thirty years.

My sisters aren't talking to each other either. One of them is still mad because the other didn't show up when she went into the hospital for a heart operation.

Grudges are something I try to avoid. They are at the top of the list of ways I tell myself I will not be like my parents. The list includes not obsessing about the past. Not requiring other people to act the way I think they should. Not judging people based on their appearance. Well, two out of four aren't bad, right?

IN THE COOLING TWILIGHT

Thirty—the promise of a decade of loneliness, a thinning list of single men to know, a thinning briefcase of enthusiasm, thinning hair…so we drove on toward death in the cooling twilight (*The Great Gatsby*).

I remember thirty; I was young then. I wasn't even married. I had girlfriends. I drank to excess and stayed up late. Weekends I played basketball with teenagers. What was Fitzgerald talking about? He was twenty-seven when he wrote those lines. He was just guessing. He went on to live to the ripe old age of forty-four when his excesses caught up with him. I've just turned sixty. By the time you're sixty you've come face to face with fate. For my midlife crises I took a leave of absence a few years ago from my day job teaching at a small liberal arts college to take a stab at my life-long dream of writing. After six months of life as a starving artist, I picked up a job teaching at a private high school.

My sister-in-law is sixty. She just retired from her position as head of human resources at a major accounting firm. She's in search of more satisfying, less time-consuming work. She's been volunteering in a women's prison and taking courses in religious studies. Like many sixty-year -olds, she wants to change her fate.

At forty you are middle-aged. What are you at sixty? Old? Not quite yet. This is not "The End" Jim Morrison sang about, but the end looms, somewhere off in the distance. It looks closer than it is, like a full moon behind the trees on a clear night. It makes you consider what you are doing, how you are spending your time. If you are sick of your job, you are already planning on what you can do when you retire. If there's something else you've always wanted to do, this could be your chance to do it. This could be your final opportunity to start your own business. If you're unhappily married, you're ready to get a divorce. If you hate your car, you're going to trade it in for the convertible, or the jeep, or the motorcycle.

At sixty we drive on toward death in the cooling twilight. It won't be long until we "rage, rage against the dying of the light." But that's because our night vision is going. What else? We need reading glasses. We have injuries that never entirely heal, phantom pains in damp weather, remaining hair turning gray, slow thinking and slower reactions, the inability to focus on multiple tasks, waning sex drive, memory loss. No wonder males over fifty commit suicide more than any other group.

Women attempt it more but men are more successful. Women favor pills. They'd rather be discovered. Guys go for guns. Say you decide you can't change your fate, that the bed you've made is a mess. You can't sleep in it, never mind lie in it. The walls of the room are closing in, the air unfit to breath and the living? Better off without you. So, you take out the revolver you keep locked up downstairs and place the barrel against your temple. One more reason not to keep a gun in the house...

By sixty you are who you are. Americans are obsessed with identity. Adolescents work overtime to establish their individuality. They rely heavily on appearance. They need piercings and tattoos and orange hair to distinguish their tribe. We become who we are in our thirties and forties; by sixty, we are there. This means that when you are sixty there is no more lying. I don't mean lying to others but lying to yourself. Bill Clinton knows that he is rake. He's trying to make up for it by helping others, especially Hillary.

Numbers say those of us in our sixties will witness the death of one, or even both of our parents soon. My father is mid-eighties. My mother died last year of heart failure. My wife's parents, have both passed away. Just staying healthy has become a challenge. One brother-in-law has diabetes. Another has chronic back pain from lymphoma. My sister never fully recovered from breast cancer. My wife was diagnosed with leukemia last fall. She was treated with chemo and it is in remission, thank God.

Isn't that a good reason to begin living a healthier life? To start, you could cut down on the booze. You can't drink anymore anyway. More than two drinks and you can't sleep. You can't drink and drive. If you do you may forget to turn your lights on. Since you can't see as well at night, you drive too slowly or you take the exit too fast and let me tell you something, there is nothing more embarrassing than getting pulled over for drinking and driving at this stage in life. I got pulled over last year when I had three beers (watching the NCAA play-offs with a friend at a local bar). I wasn't drunk but the cop (who couldn't have been more than twelve years old) wouldn't believe me. He had my car towed. It was only after I took a breathalyzer at the station that they let me go. I slunk home and paid eighty bucks to retrieve my car the next morning.

You could step up the exercise. You see a lot of people over sixty running and playing tennis and going to the gym. One in four of us exercise regularly, a figure that has remained constant over the last two decades. I run three or four times a week. I ran a marathon last spring but I had to walk the last six miles. It took me four and a half hours. If I were running to warn the Athenians, the city would be under siege by the time I got there. I also lift weights for twenty minutes two or three days a week. I try to do this around five in the afternoon but if I am tired or don't feel like it, I skip it and have a beer instead.

A few years ago on a whim I decided to try snowboarding under the impression that it would be easier on my knees than skiing. It turns out that snowboarding is easier on the knees and is a lot of fun. There are, however, a couple of minor drawbacks. For one thing, you fall all the time. Where it is okay to fall when you are ten, twenty, even thirty, a fall at sixty can result in nagging injuries. I sprained my wrist on New Year's Day and it was two months before I could lift weights again. And although snowboarding is easier on the knees, it's harder on the back. I had to be taken down the mountain on a rescue sled last winter when my back went out. It was kind of fun but really embarrassing.

The other problem is not with snowboarding itself but with what it brings to light and that is: the fear. Don't tell anyone about this because it is a secret among guys, but the fear begins to sneak up on you in your forties and by the time you're sixty, it has taken up residence in your house. I know because fifteen years ago, I painted my house. I bought a nice twenty-eight-foot fiberglass ladder so I could reach the eaves. I used to work as a painter in summers when I was in college and I know what I'm doing but whenever I climbed up on that ladder, I had to psych myself up. I'd get nervous up there. I could see the headlines: "Man Plunges to Death While Painting House." "Man Blown Off

Ladder." Or worse: "Man Rescued From Ladder by Local Fire Department."

The other problem with snowboarding is that snowboarders do jumps. The little jumps, one or two feet high are fine but my son, who is twenty, likes to do the big jumps, the ten and fifteen footers which are giant white cliffs of snow created by the deranged men who groom the slopes at night. In my mind's eye I can make these jumps. I was a gymnast in high school, but when I try them now, I often fall down on purpose while approaching take-off. If I happen to make the jump I usually fall afterward in a wimpy attempt to slow down.

Better I fall than my son. If anything happens to him, I may start weeping. I've become very emotional, very sensitive. I often find myself choking up watching television shows or movies or reading novels. Newspaper stories can also make me lose it. Old photos? Forget about it. In short, I've become sentimental. Of course, this is better than being the callous, devil-may-care fool I was in my twenties but it is a bit unnerving.

Okay I'm being disingenuous. For one thing, it's much better than I thought it would be. I am, after all, able to run; I do lift weights, and snowboard. I also know what's good in wine, food, books, magazines, movies. And early mornings I seem to be able to see more clearly than ever how the light strikes the trees, illuminates the grass and infiltrates the water. The sunsets seem to be getting better, and I don't mind hearing the song sparrow outside my window at five am because I'm already awake anyway. I guess you could call turning sixty a mixed bag which is better than being an old bag.

Perhaps the Russians had the right idea. In Chekhov's plays, a man of sixty is in his prime—at the top of his career—ready to settle down and marry. I've read personals that say: Sixty and fabulous. Some older women do look great. There's Cher Surgery, Goldie-still-cute-Hawn, Susan-still-sexy-Sarandon.

Maybe science will rescue us. Bill Nye was right when he claimed, "science rules." Science now operates outside anyone's control. That could be good news for us in terms of longevity, replacement parts, memory enhancement and cures for many of the diseases that plague person-kind. Evidently, we'll leave the next generation to deal with implanting computer chips, genetic manipulation, cyborgs and clone clans. I'm against anything that makes us less human, but in another thirty years when my son will be dealing with those changes, I won't have anything to say about it. I'll be enjoying the big sleep.

WELLFLEET

"It's not what you look at, it's what you see." --Thoreau

"I am the monarch of all I survey." --Cowper

Walking out of my house in Wellfleet I cross the street and follow a sandy horse-trail that weaves through my neighbor's place. Oak and maple trees create a canopy over my head--a cool tunnel even in the middle of the summer. Bearberry, sheep laurel and scrub oak brush my ankles as I walk.

In a little less than a mile the trail opens onto Cahoon Hollow, a narrow road that snakes down to dunes and National Seashore. Across the road is Great Pond, a formed by the last glacier when it retreated 12,000 years ago. Great Pond is about a third of a mile across and almost perfectly round. There's a wooden stairway down to the water and a narrow beach of white sand at the bottom of the stairs. The water is cool in May and June but it warms up in the summer and stays in the 70s until October. The bottom of the pond is sandy and the water is clear and pure so when you swim you can see the sand until you are well over your head.

During the summer, my wife and I swim here or in one of the other ponds nearby almost every day. If you follow the fire road that runs alongside Great Pond for half a mile you'll come to Dyer Pond; its claim to fame is a rope swing suspended from a tree. If you keep going you'll soon get to Long Pond—a favorite of families with its beach and parking. All the ponds are technically lakes because they have little vegetation growing in them; all of them are beautiful, especially at the end of the day when the light filters through the pines and glimmers off the scrub oak leaves to prance along the water.

When it gets hot, we head to the beach. There are beaches on both sides of the cape. On the Outer Banks the harbor and the ocean are only a couple of miles apart. The beaches on the harbor side are family friendly with small waves and easy access. Since they face west, they are a great place to watch the sunset. But the best beaches are on the ocean side.

About a mile east on Cahoon Hollow from Great Pond, the road intersects with Ocean View Drive. If you go straight across, you plunge downhill to Cahoon Hollow beach where the Beachcomber Bar sits atop a plateau of sand and a steep trail cuts down the dunes to the shore. Cahoon Hollow draws the crowds but the best, most spectacular beach is about a mile north.

White Crest Beach sits at the bottom of 75 foot dunes. Each year a new trail has to be carved by beachgoers since the ocean and wind wash and blow the trail away during the winter. The trail cuts diagonally down to the beach. It's an easy lope down but a challenging climb back up. At its base is an expanse of white and ochre sand where you can watch the ocean roll in on two to four foot waves. For the last few summers, seals have been trolling by and there have been a few Great White shark sightings.

A number of houses that sit precariously atop the cliffs on Ocean View have been moved back away from the dunes in the past twenty-five years. Last year, the Beachcomber lost half its shore-side parking lot to winter storms.

The ocean is usually cold. Stay in long and the numbness works its way up from your toes. It's refreshing though when the temperature gets into the 80s. It can be rough with an undertow, but at low tide it's great for body surfing, boogie boarding and for surfers skilled enough to pop up and ride the fast breaking waves diagonally. It never gets crowded at White Crest. There's plenty of room to set up horseshoes or play whiffle-ball or tag football.

The roads in Wellfleet are narrow and hilly so the Outer Banks is a spectacular place to ride a bike although drivers of cars need to be patient. They usually are. I like to take a ten mile route that circles around Great Pond to Long Pond and up Gross Hill to Ocean View past Gull Pond. You can also follow the harbor out Chequessett Road on rolling hills that pass beautiful houses that perch on the hill and peer out at the bay.

If it's not too hot, and my knees are up to it, I like to jog on the trails that run through the woods past the ponds to Long Pond Road, up the big hill and then along the ocean and back through the woods to my house. There I'll take an outdoor shower followed by a beer, fresh fish on the grill and dinner on the deck. I keep the feeders full and watch blue jays, cardinals, rock doves, and chickadees fly in for free food. In June, bluebirds and Baltimore Orioles stop by. If we're lucky hummingbirds helicopter in to sip sugar water.

What happens when you're immersed in such a beautiful environment is that time begins to change its shape. The straight line of the digital clock fades into the background of trail walks and swims in crystal clear water and late-afternoon light flashing through trees while shadows crawl across ponds. Eventually you begin to feel as if you are part of the natural world and that world exudes a certain power. Part of that power everyone recognizes as reducing stress, allowing you to relax but it goes beyond that. It's effortlessly rewarding. You don't have to work at it, you can just accept it as a gift. That gift is uplifting in a way that has nothing to do with organized religion but is intimately tied to spirituality.

I imagine this is what I'll miss when I'm no longer here—on earth I mean. But I can live with that as long as I know it will be here for those that follow after I'm gone.

Acknowledgements

"Headmaster," *Rivanna Review*; "Love and Affection," *The Christian Science Monitor*; "Reading Aloud," *The Bad Day Parenting Book*; "Fifth Grade Dance," *The Patriot Ledger*; "The Alliance," *The Boston Sunday Globe Magazine*; "Until the End," *Fathom Magazine*; "In the Cooling Twilight," *Getting Old*; "Melody Edwardson," *Rivanna Review*; "Wellfleet," *Thorn and Bloom*.

THE AUTHOR

Ed Meek is the author of *High Tide* and three other books of poetry, and *Luck*, a collection of short stories. He has had work in *The Sun, The Paris Review, Plume, The North American Review, The Boston Globe*. He writes book reviews for *The Arts Fuse*. He teaches creative writing at the Osher Lifelong Learning Institute. He lives in Great Barrington with his wife Elizabeth and their labradoodle Mookie.